Herbert Puchta and Jeff Stranks

English in Mind

* **Student's Book Starter**

CAMBRIDGE
UNIVERSITY PRESS

	Unit	Grammar	Vocabulary	Pronunciation
Module 1 **Me and others**	1 I know!	*What's … ?* Plurals. *a & an.*	International words. Classroom objects. Adjectives & opposites. The alphabet. Numbers 0–100.	Word stress.
	2 She isn't American	The verb *be* (singular): statements & questions. Question words: *who, what, how old, where?*	Countries & nationalities.	*from.*
	3 We're a new band	The verb *be* (plural): negatives & questions. *I (don't) like / Do you like?* Object pronouns.	Positive & negative adjectives.	/ɪ/ & /iː/
	4 She likes Harry Potter	Present simple: positive & negative, questions & short answers. Possessive *'s*; possessive adjectives.	Family.	/s/, /z/ & /ɪz/
	Module 1 Check your progress			
Module 2 **People and places**	5 Where's the cafe?	*there's / there are.* Positive imperatives. Prepositions of place.	Places in towns. Numbers 100 +.	/ð/ & /θ/
	6 They've got brown eyes	*has / have got* *why … ? because …*	Colours. Parts of the body.	/v/ *they've*
	7 This is delicious!	*I'd like / Would you like … ?* Countable & uncountable nouns. *this / that / these / those*	Food.	/w/ *would*
	8 I sometimes watch soaps	Present simple with adverbs of frequency.	Days of the week. TV programmes. Telling the time.	Compound nouns.
	Module 2 Check your progress			
Module 3 **Free time**	9 Don't close the door!	Negative imperatives.	Adjectives to describe feelings.	Linking sounds.
	10 We can't lose	*can / can't* (ability) *like / don't like -ing.*	Sports.	*can & can't.*
	11 Reading on the roof!	Present continuous.	House & furniture.	/h/ *have*
	12 Can I try them on?	*can / can't* (asking for permission). Prepositions of time. *one / ones.*	Months of the year & seasons. Clothes.	/æ/ & /e/
	Module 3 Check your progress			
Module 4 **Past and present**	13 He was only 40	Past simple: *was / wasn't & were / weren't.*	Time expressions. Ordinal numbers & dates.	*was / wasn't & were / weren't.*
	14 She didn't listen	Past simple: regular verbs, questions & negatives.	Verb & noun pairs.	*-ed* endings.
	15 Where did they go?	Past simple: irregular verbs.	Adverbs.	Adverbs.
	16 Now and then	Comparison of adjectives.	Adjectives & opposites.	/ðən/ *than*
	Module 4 Check your progress			
	Projects • Irregular verbs and phonetics • Wordlist			

Speaking & functions	Listening	Reading	Writing
Spelling words. Exchanging phone numbers. Using classroom language.	International words. Classroom objects. The alphabet. Phone numbers.	Story: No problem.	Phone message.
Talking about nationalities & countries. Asking questions. Correcting information.	A game show.	Dialogue in a game show. Culture: Heroes and heroines.	Information about yourself.
Expressing likes & dislikes. Describing nouns.	People talking about things they like & don't like.	Interview with a singer. Story: They all want to go …	Email about your favourite band.
Talking about your family. Asking questions about habits.	Dialogue about a family.	A famous writer. Culture: British families.	Paragraph about your family.
Asking for & giving directions. Saying where things are.	People giving directions.	A great trip to London! Story: I have no idea!	Short text about your town or city.
Talking about things you've got. Describing people. Giving personal information.	Descriptions of people.	Sally or Paula? Culture: Pets in the UK.	Descriptions of friends or family members.
Ordering food in a restaurant. Talking about food.	Dialogues in a shop and a restaurant.	Would you like our special? Story: I'm really hungry!	Letter to a host family.
Talking about regular activities & daily routine. Interviewing people about TV.	Times. Interviews about TV & TV programmes.	Different lives. Culture: What British teenagers watch.	Paragraph about TV.
Describing feelings. Giving orders.	A story. A song.	Letter to a boyfriend. Story: I miss San Francisco.	Email about your friends & school.
Talking about ability.	Information about abilities of people & animals. Dialogue about sports.	We never win but we always win. Culture: Sport in British schools.	Email about sports you do.
Talking about present activities. Describing a house.	Listen to sounds & describe activities.	Dialogue about present activities. Story: I'm on my way!	Postcard to a friend.
Talking about dates & seasons. Describing people's clothes. Discussing clothes & shopping. Asking for permission.	Descriptions of what people are wearing. Shopping dialogues.	Americans love to party! Dialogues in a clothes shop. Culture: London's carnival.	Email about a festival.
Talking about past situations. Talking about dates.	Dialogue about the Beatles. Dates.	There was a man at the door. Story: Rob's wallet.	Email about a holiday.
Questionnaire about past activities.	Radio quiz about past events.	The lady with the lamp. Culture: Steve Biko – a South African hero.	Paragraph for school magazine about a famous person.
Re-telling a story. Making guesses about past or present situations.	Radio interview about Lord Lucan.	The mystery of Lord Lucan. A mystery at sea. Story: Who's Caroline?	Story about a strange place.
Describing things. Comparing people, places & objects.	Dialogue comparing life now & in the past.	Island chef cooks in L.A. Culture: UK holiday camps – then and now.	Competition entry.

Welcome!

1 🔊 Listen and read

Rob: Hi! I'm Rob. What's your name?

Amy: I'm Amy, and this is Lucy.

Alex: Hello. My name's Alex.

2 Speak

Work in small groups. Say your name.

A: *Hi! I'm _____ . What's your name?*

B: *Hello, my name's _____ , and this is _____ .*

Module 1
Me and others

YOU WILL LEARN ABOUT ...

- International words   _1_
- Famous people
- Countries and nationalities
- A famous writer
- British families

⁕ Can you match each photo with a topic?

YOU WILL LEARN HOW TO ...

Speak
- Introduce yourself
- Ask for words in English
- Talk about famous people
- Interview a partner about the things they like
- Interview a partner about J.K. Rowling and Harry Potter
- Interview a partner about the things they do
- Talk about your family

Write
- A telephone message
- A letter about yourself
- An email about your favourite band
- A paragraph about your family

Read
- A dialogue in a game show
- An interview with a singer
- An article about a famous writer
- An article about families in Britain

Listen
- A telephone message
- A game show
- Information about famous people
- A dialogue about someone's family

Use grammar

Can you match the names of the grammar points with the examples?

Plurals	This is **Peter's** book.
The verb *be*	I really like **them**!
Question words	She's here in England with **her** family.
like / don't like	He **studies** French at school.
Object pronouns	Nick and Mike **are** 17.
Present simple	Two **men** and three **cats**.
Possessive *'s*	**Where** are you from?
Possessive adjectives	I **don't like** Ricky Martin.

Use vocabulary

Can you think of two more examples for each topic?

Classroom objects	Adjectives	Nationalities	Family
pencil	expensive	English	parents
cassette	small	Italian	sister
....	....	....	....
....	....	....	....

1 I know!

* *What's ... in English?*
* Plurals; *a* and *an*
* Vocabulary: international words; classroom objects;
  adjectives and opposites; the alphabet; numbers 0–100

1 Read and listen

a Match the words with the pictures. Write 1–12 in the boxes.

museum ☐ TV ☐ phone ☐ pizza ☐ sandwich ☐ restaurant ☐ city [1] taxi ☐
football ☐ hamburger ☐ video ☐ hotel ☐

1

2

3

4

5

6

7

8

9

10

11

12

b 🔊 Listen, check and repeat.

2 Vocabulary
Classroom objects

a Look at the pictures. Ask the teacher: 'What's ... in English?'

1 _____pen_____   2 _____   3 _____   4 _____   5 _____

6 _____   7 _____   8 _____   9 _____   10 _____

b 🔊 Write words from the box under the pictures in Exercise 2a. Listen, check and repeat.

> ~~pen~~ notebook book cassette pencil desk board
> window door chair

c Work with a partner. Ask and answer questions about the pictures.

A: *What's ... in English?*
B: *It's a desk.*

Look

Singular	Plural
one man	three (3) men
one woman	two (2) women
one **person**	six (6) **people**

---

3 Grammar
Plurals

Write the words under the pictures.

1 _____2 pens_____   2 _____   3 _____

4 _____   5 _____   6 _____

---

4 Pronunciation
Word stress

a 🔊 Listen and repeat the words in the table.

A	B	C
read	open	computer
cheap	teacher	cinema
desk	hotel	hamburger

b 🔊 Listen and write the words under A, B or C.

5 Vocabulary
Adjectives

a Write words from the box under the pictures.

> a big TV   an old man   a new book   a small hotel   a bad singer
> an interesting film   ~~a cheap computer~~   a good hamburger

1 _a cheap computer_   2 ....

3 ....   4 ....

5 ....   6 ....

7 ....   8 ....

b Listen, check and repeat.

c Put the words in the correct order.

1 city / big / a
   a big city ....

2 CD / good / a
   ....

3 restaurant / an / expensive
   ....

4 interesting / museum / an
   ....

5 football / good / team / a
   ....

6 game / an / interesting / computer
   ....
   ....

Look

a **b**ig restaurant
a **g**ood teacher
an **e**xpensive hotel
an **i**nteresting film

d Give examples from Exercise 5c.

a big city   *Tokyo*

e Match the opposites.

good   interesting
big   new
boring   bad
old   small
cheap   expensive

6 Listen

a 🔊 Listen to the alphabet. Then listen and repeat.

A a	J j	S s
B b	K k	T t
C c	L l	U u
D d	M m	V v
E e	N n	W w
F f	O o	X x
G g	P p	Y y
H h	Q q	Z z
I i	R r	

b Write the letters of the alphabet under the correct sounds.

/e/	/eɪ/	/iː/	/aɪ/	/əʊ/	/uː/	/ɑː/
f	a	b	i	o	q	r

c 🔊 Listen, check and repeat.

d Think of a famous person. Spell his or her name for your partner.

M-A-D-O-N-N-A

7 Vocabulary

Numbers 0–20

a 🔊 Look at the numbers 0–20. Listen and repeat.

0	zero / 'oh'	11	eleven
1	one	12	twelve
2	two	13	thirteen
3	three	14	fourteen
4	four	15	fifteen
5	five	16	sixteen
6	six	17	seventeen
7	seven	18	eighteen
8	eight	19	nineteen
9	nine	20	twenty
10	ten		

b Listen to your teacher. Tick (✓) the numbers you hear.

c 🔊 Listen and write down the phone numbers you hear.

1 .... 3 ....

2 .... 4 ....

d Ask and answer.

A: *What's your phone number?*
B: *It's* ....

Numbers 20–100

e 🔊 Listen and repeat the numbers.

20	twenty	70	seventy
30	thirty	80	eighty
40	forty	90	ninety
50	fifty	100	a hundred
60	sixty		

f 🔊 How do you say these numbers? Listen, check and repeat.

1	26	4	47
2	29	5	58
3	35	6	64

No problem

8 Read and listen

a) 🔊 Read and listen to the photo story.

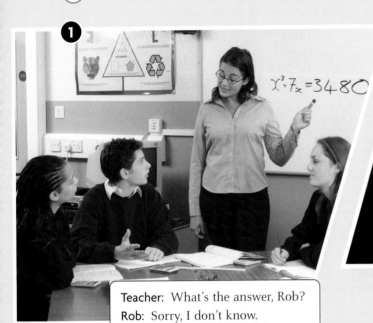

1

$$x^3 + 7_x = 3480$$

Teacher: What's the answer, Rob?
Rob: Sorry, I don't know.

2

$$x^3 + 7_x = 3480$$

Lucy: I know, Miss. Fifteen.
Teacher: That's right, Lucy. Excellent!

3

Rob: I don't understand.
Amy: No problem, Rob. I can help you.

4

Amy: OK?
Rob: Yes, great. Thanks, Amy.

b Match the names with the faces. Write the names in the spaces.

> Lucy   Rob
> Amy

(1)

(2)

(3)

----

9 Everyday English

a Make sentences.

I	the answer?
What's	right.
I don't	know.
No	understand.
That's	problem.

b How do you say these things in your language?

1 Sorry, I don't know.
2 I know.
3 I don't understand.
4 Excellent.
5 OK?
6 Yes, great.
7 Thanks.
8 I can help you.

10 Listen and write

a 🔊 Listen to the message and read the note to Lucy.

> Lucy!
>
> Message from Mrs Hurley on 01433 651464.
>
> The homework's on page 78.

b 🔊 Now listen and complete the message to Rob.

> Rob!
>
> Message from Mrs _____ .
> The homework's on page _____ .
> Phone number _____ .

② She isn't American

* The verb *be* (singular): statements and questions
* Question words: *who, what, how old, where?*
* Vocabulary: countries and nationalities

1 Read and listen

(a) 🔊 Read and listen to the game show. Who's the winner?

Host: Hello, and welcome to *Who's the star?* And your names are …?

Carol: Hello. I'm Carol Wilcox, from London.

Jonathan: Hi, I'm Jonathan Smith, and I'm from Cambridge.

Host: Carol, star number one, please!

Carol: OK. Star number one's a man. He's a football player.

Jonathan: Is he Spanish?

Carol: Yes, he is.

Jonathan: Raúl González?

Host: Yes! Great. Six points for Carol, and six points for Jonathan. Now Jonathan.

Jonathan: OK. Star number two's a woman. She's American.

Carol: Is she a tennis player?

Jonathan: No, she isn't.

Carol: Is she an actor?

Jonathan: Yes, she is.

Carol: Nicole Kidman?

Host: OK! Six points for Carol. Sorry, Jonathan. Only four points for you. Nicole Kidman isn't American, she's Australian.

b 🔊 Who are the stars? Match the names with the pictures. Write the names in the spaces. Then listen and check.

Ricky Martin   Jennifer Lopez
Kim Clijsters   Luciano Pavarotti

 1

 2

 3

 4

....

2 Grammar

The verb *be* (singular)

a Look at the examples.

I'm Carol Wilcox.   ***Is** she a tennis player?*   *You're the winner.*   *She **isn't** American.*

b Complete the table.

Positive	Negative	Question	Short answer Positive / Negative
I'm (I am).	I'm not (I am not).	Am I?	Yes, I **am**. / No, I'm **not**.
You .... (You **are**).	You **aren't** (You **are not**).	.... you?	Yes, you .... / No, you ....
He's (He **is**).	He **isn't** (He **is not**).	.... he?	Yes, he .... / No, he **isn't**.
She .... (She **is**).	She .... (She **is not**).	.... she?	Yes, she .... / No, she ....
It .... (It **is**).	It .... (It **is not**).	.... it?	Yes, it .... / No, it ....

c Write *'m, 're* or *'s* in the spaces.

1   I .... an actor, not a tennis player.
2   He .... a film star, not a footballer.
3   You .... right, Sue. Good!
4   She .... a great teacher.

d Write negative sentences.

1   He's from Italy.   *He isn't from Italy.*
2   She's a film star. ....
3   You're the winner. ....
4   I'm a tennis player. ....

e Write words from the box in the spaces to make questions.

Is   Are   Am   Is

1   .... I right?
2   .... you OK?
3   .... he the winner?
4   .... it a big hotel?

f Work with a partner. Ask and answer questions from the box.

How old are you? I'm ....
My sister's 16. My best friend is 17.

How old is your sister?
          brother?
          best friend?

Look

You **are** ....
Are you .... ?

3 Vocabulary

Countries

a 🔊 Listen and repeat the names of the countries.

• Spain •• Belgium •• Britain •• Poland •• Brazil ••• Switzerland

b 🔊 Listen and write the words from the box in the table.

China Russia Turkey Italy Canada Germany Japan

• •	• •	• • •
China		

c Work with a partner. Match the numbers in the map with the countries in Exercise 3.

Number one's _____ . Is number two _____ ?

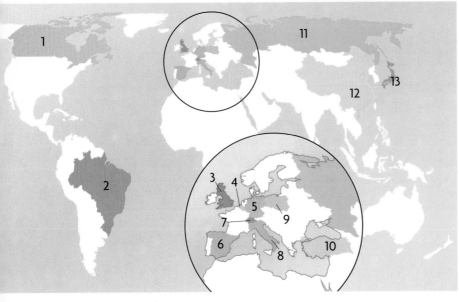

d 🔊 Listen and check.

e Match the words for the countries with the pictures.

I think number one's in _____ .

Japan Italy Brazil
Britain Turkey Poland

4 Grammar

Where are you from?

a 🔊 Listen and write the words in the spaces.

Hi! I'm Andrea. I'm from ¹ _____ .

Hi, Andrea. ² _____ Tomasz.

Where are you ³ _____ , Tomasz?

_____ .

b Complete the sentences.

1 I _____ from Poland.
2 Where _____ you from?
3 He's _____ England.

5 Pronunciation

from

a 🔊 Listen again to the sentences in Exercise 4a. Listen to the word *from*. Is it the same in both the sentences?

b 🔊 Listen again and repeat.

6 Vocabulary

Nationalities

a Write nationality adjectives in the table.

> ~~Italy~~ Turkey   Britain   ~~Poland~~
> Brazil Belgium   ~~China~~   Japan
> Russia   Canada   Spain   Portugal

-an	*-ish*	*-ese*
Italian	*Polish*	*Chinese*

b 🔊 Listen, check and repeat.

c Write the nationalities below the flags.

> Turkish   British   Belgian   Russian
> Brazilian   Italian   Chinese   Polish

d Work with a partner.

I think number ...... is the Italian flag.
What's number ...... ?

e 🔊 Listen and check your answers.

Look

an Italian actor / **a** Polish singer /
a Turkish writer

7 Grammar

wh- question words

a How do you say these question words in your language?

What? Where? Who? How?

b Write the question words from Exercise 7a in the spaces.

1 A: ___What___'s this?
   B: It's an Italian flag.

2 A: _____ are you from?
   B: I'm from Rome.

3 A: _____'s this in English?
   B: It's a book.

4 A: _____'s your school?
   B: It's here, in Milan.

5 A: _____ old are you?
   B: I'm 13.

6 A: _____'s this (girl)?
   B: She's my friend.

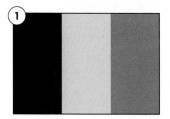

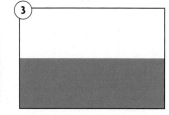

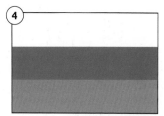

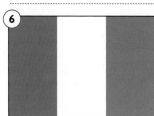

Culture in mind

Heroes and heroines

Venus Williams

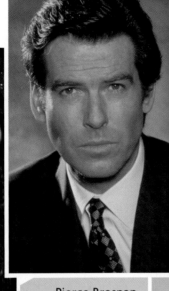
Pierce Brosnan

Alicia Keys

Gisele Bundchen

Zinedine Zidane

Annika Sorenstam

Enrique Iglesias

8 Speak

Work with a partner. Talk about the people on page 18. Use the information in the table.

Zidane's a football player. **He's from** Marseille. **He's** French.

1 ... ~~a football player.~~	... Madrid.	... Brazilian.
2 ... a model.	... Horizontina.	... Irish.
3 ... a singer.	... California.	... American.
4 ... a tennis player.	... Navan, County Meath.	... American.
5 ... a singer.	... ~~Marseille.~~	... Spanish.
6 ... an actor.	... New York.	... ~~French.~~
7 ... a golfer.	... Stockholm.	... Swedish.

9 Listen

a 🔊 Listen and check your answers to Exercise 8.

b Correct the information. Write the correct answers.

1 Pierce Brosnan is a football player. *No, he isn't, he's an actor.*
2 Venus Williams is from Barcelona. _____
3 Alicia Keys is from Los Angeles. _____
4 Enrique Iglesias is American. _____
5 Zinedine Zidane is a golfer. _____
6 Gisele Bundchen is from Rio de Janeiro. _____
7 Annika Sorenstam is from Norway. _____

c Who is your hero or heroine?

10 Writing

a Read the example. Where is Joanna from? How old is she? Who is her heroine?

Hi! I'm Joanna. I'm 14. I'm English.
I'm from Manchester. My address is
4 Brooklands Road, Sale, Manchester.
My mobile phone number is 07715
201523. My heroine is Alicia Keys.
She's from New York.

This isn't Alicia, this is me!

b Now write about yourself. Use Joanna's text to help you.

Hi!

(3) We're a new band

* The verb *be* (plural): negatives and questions
* *I (don't) like ... / Do you like ... ?*
* Object pronouns
* Vocabulary: positive and negative adjectives

1 Read and listen

a Which bands are popular in your country? Who are the popular singers?

b 🔊 Nick is in a band called 4Tune. Read and listen to the interview. Then answer the questions.

1 How many people are in the band?
2 Where are they from?

Zoë: Hi, Nick. Welcome to the show. You're the singer with 4Tune.

Nick: Hi, Zoë. That's right, we're a new band.

Zoë: Are you all from Cambridge?

Nick: No, we aren't. I'm from Cambridge, but the other three are from London.

Zoë: OK. And how old are you?

Nick: I'm 17, and Mike, Karen and Melanie are all 19.

Zoë: OK. And Nick – you're very popular in Cambridge ...

Nick: *Very* popular? Well, thanks Zoë, but we aren't very popular!

Zoë: Well, the band plays great music, and here's their new song, *They Say I'm Lucky.*

c Mark the statements *T* (true) or *F* (false).

1 Zoë is the singer. ☐
2 The band are all from Cambridge. ☐
3 Nick and Mike are 17. ☐
4 4Tune are a popular band. ☐
5 *They Say I'm Lucky* is 4Tune's new song. ☐

2 Grammar

The verb *be*: plural, negatives and questions

a Look at the examples.

We're a new band.   We aren't very popular.   Are you all from Cambridge?

b Complete the table.

Positive	Negative	Question	Short answer Positive / Negative
You're (You are).	You aren't.	Are you?	Yes, you............ . / No, you ....
We .... (We are).	We	............we?	Yes, we............ . / No, we ....
They .... (They are).	They	.... they?	Yes, they............ . / No, they ....

c Write the correct words in the spaces.

1 Adnan: ...*Are*... they American?

   Eda: No, they ....
   They .... British.

2 Mum: .... you and Dave OK?

   Alex: No, we ....

3 Arne: .... you from China?

   Girl: No, we .... We .... from Japan.

d Complete the sentences.

1 A: Is Simon Australian?

   B: No, I think ...*he's*... British.

2 A: Is *Juno* a good film?

   B: No, ... very interesting.

3 A: U2? .... they a pop group?

   B: Yes, ... great!

4 A: .... Pietro and Daniela from Italy?

   B: No, ... Italian, they're Swiss.

e Look at the pictures and complete the questions.

1 .....*Is*..... Sydney the capital of Australia?
2 .... the Backstreet Boys from the USA?
3 .... Luis Figo French?
4 .... Victoria and David Beckham American?
5 .... the Taj Mahal in India?
6 .... Hyundai a Japanese company?

3 Vocabulary

Positive and negative adjectives

(a) Look at the words in the box. Do the words mean 'very good' or 'very bad'?

> fantastic wonderful
> awful terrible great

(b) Work with a partner. Make sentences. Use words from the box.

I think Rome is a fantastic city.

> a fantastic city
> a terrible CD
> a great band
> an awful video
> a wonderful team
> a terrible film

4 Grammar and speaking

I (don't) like ... / Do you like ... ?

(a) Write verbs from the box in the table.

> I like (Busted)   I don't like (Ricky Martin)

| ☺ _____ | ☹ _____ |

(b) Who do you like? Write your answers.

A singer I like: _____
A band I don't like: _____
My favourite band: _____
My favourite singer: _____

Question	Short answer	Statement	Negative
Do you like ... ?	Yes, I do. No, I don't (do not).	I like ...	I don't like ...

(c) Work with a partner. Say your answers to Exercise 4b.

I like (Busted).   I don't like (Kylie).   I don't like (U2).
My favourite band's (Orange).

(d) Work with a partner. Ask and answer questions. Use the words from the box and from Exercise 3a.

A: *Do you like football?*
B: *No, I don't. It's terrible. Do you like volleyball?*
A: *Yes, I do. It's my favourite sport! Do you like cats?*
B: *No, I don't. They're awful!*

> football   chocolate   coffee   jam   cats
> classical music   dogs   horses   volleyball

5 Grammar

Object pronouns

a ◁)) Read and listen to the dialogue.

A: *Here's the new Robbie Williams CD. Do you like him?*
B: *He's OK. My favourite singer is Madonna.*
A: *I don't like her.*

b Write the words from the box in the table.

~~you~~	her	it	them	us	me	him

Subject:	I	you	she	he	it	we	they
Object:	......	*you*	......	......	......	......	......

c Complete the sentences with words from Exercise 5b.

1 Mr Brown is awful. I don't like .... at all.
2 Coldplay are my favourite band. I really like .... !
3 Britney Spears is a good singer. I like .... a lot.
4 We like Joan and Anna, but they don't like ....

6 Pronunciation

/ɪ/ and /iː/

a ◁)) Listen to the two words.

big   three

b Write the words from the box in the table.

big /ɪ/	three /iː/
....	....
....	....
....	....
....	....

six	he	we	it	city	cheap	video
fourteen						

c ◁)) Listen, check and repeat.

7 Listen and speak

a ◁)) Listen to four people talking about the people or things in the photos. Write the names under the correct columns in the table.

	Like ☺	Don't like ☹
Speaker 1	*Manchester United*	
Speaker 2	....	....
Speaker 3	....	....
Speaker 4	....	....

U2

Manchester United

Tom Cruise

Christina Aguilera

Pelé

Salma Hayek

b Work with a partner. Talk about stars you really like or don't like.

A: *Do you like Christina Aguilera?*
B: *Yes, I really like her. I think she's fantastic. Do you like Tom Cruise?*
A: *No, I don't. I think he's awful.*

They all want to go ...

8 Read and listen

(a) 🔊 Look at the title of the photo story and the pictures.
Who wants to go to the concert? Read, listen and check your answer.

1

Amy: Listen Lucy! 4Tune are at our school
on Friday.

Lucy: 4Tune? Who are they?

Amy: My friend Nick's band. They're really
great. Do you want to come? Let's go together.

Lucy: No, thanks.

2

Amy: Oh, hi, Alex. ... Yes, isn't it
fantastic? ... Of course I want to go!
What about you? ... Great! See you all
on Friday, then. Bye.

3

Amy: Guess what? Alex, Chris and Mark
all want to go to the concert!

Lucy: Hmmm. I think I want to go, too.

(b) Look at the story again. Mark the statements *T* (true) or *F* (false).

1 4Tune are at the school on Friday. ☐
2 Amy thinks 4Tune are awful. ☐
3 Amy wants to go to the concert with Lucy. ☐
4 Mark is on the phone. ☐

9 Everyday English

a Find the expressions in the story. Who says them?

1 Let's go together.   3 What about you?

2 Of course I want to go!   4 Guess what?

b How do you say the expressions in Exercise 9a in your language?

c 🔊 Read the dialogue and put the sentences in the correct order. Then listen and check.

Anna: All my friends want to go. What about you? ....

Anna: So let's go together. ....

Julia: Great! I love Brad Pitt. ....

Anna: Guess what? There's a new film on at the cinema. With Brad Pitt. __1__

Julia: Of course I want to go. ....

Julia: Fantastic. I'm really excited. __6__

10 Write

a Read Anna's email about her favourite band. What is her favourite CD?

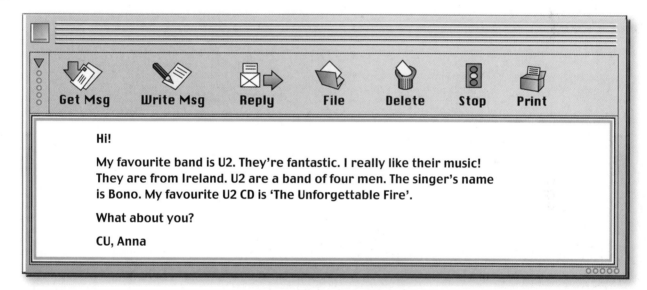

Get Msg   Write Msg   Reply   File   Delete   Stop   Print

Hi!

My favourite band is U2. They're fantastic. I really like their music!
They are from Ireland. U2 are a band of four men. The singer's name
is Bono. My favourite U2 CD is 'The Unforgettable Fire'.

What about you?

CU, Anna

b Write your friend an email about your favourite band. Tell him or her:

- the name of your favourite band.
- where they are from.
- why you like them.
- who is in the band.

4 She likes Harry Potter

* Present simple: positive and negative; questions and short answers
* Possessive *'s*; possessive adjectives
* Vocabulary: family

1 Read and listen

a Look at the photos. Who is the woman? Read the magazine article and check your answer.

b 🔊 Read the article again and listen. Mark the statements *T* (true) or *F* (false).

1 J.K. Rowling is American. ☐
2 She lives with her aunt and uncle. ☐
3 She likes cartoons. ☐
4 She doesn't have a computer. ☐
5 Harry likes his aunt and uncle. ☐
6 Harry doesn't like Hogwarts school. ☐

c Do you like Harry Potter?

A Famous Writer

J.K. Rowling is a very famous writer. Millions of children, teenagers, men and women read her books. Where is she from? Where does she live? How does she write her books?

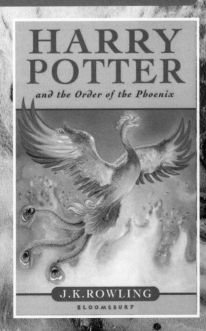

J.K. Rowling is from Britain, and she lives with her husband, son and daughter in Scotland. Writing is her hobby and her work. She always writes with a pen first, and then with her computer. She sometimes watches TV: she really likes cartoons. Harry Potter is always the hero in her books. Of course she likes him a lot!

Harry Potter is ten years old and he's very unhappy. His mother and father are dead and he lives with his aunt and uncle. Harry doesn't like them or their son Dudley at all. One day, Harry gets a letter from Hogwarts, a school for wizards! At Hogwarts, Harry is famous and popular. He learns magic and plays a game called 'Quidditch'. Harry's very happy there.

2 Grammar

Present simple: positive and negative

a Look at the sentences. <u>Underline</u> the verbs.

1 I <u>don't like</u> them.
2 I really <u>like</u> their music.
3 He <u>learns</u> magic.
4 He <u>doesn't like</u> his school.

b Complete the table.

Positive	Negative
I / you / we / they .... he / she / (it) reads.	I / you / we / they .... read. he / she / (it) .... read.

c Look at the spelling for the third person singular. Complete the table.

+s	+es	+ies
learn → learns stop → .... live → .... play →	watch → watches finish → .... go →	study → studies

d Write the correct words in the spaces.

1 I ...._like_........ the Beatles. (like)
2 We .... pizza. (not like)
3 He .... French at school. (study)
4 He .... Italian. (not speak)
5 She .... to music. (not listen)
6 I .... English. (not study)

Present simple: questions and short answers

e Look at these questions in the present simple.

Do you like them?
Do they speak Italian?
Does she have a computer?
Do you understand?

f Complete the table with *do* or *does*.

Question	Short answer	
	Positive	**Negative**
Does he/she speak Italian?	Yes, he/she	No, he/she **doesn't** (does not).
.... I/you/we/they study English?	Yes, I/you/we/they	No, I/you/we/they .... (do not).

g Complete the questions with *do* or *does*.

1 ..._Does_.. J.K. Rowling live in America?
2 .... Harry Potter live with his parents?
3 .... Harry's aunt and uncle like him?
4 .... millions of children read J.K. Rowling's books?
5 .... J.K. Rowling have a computer?

3 Pronunciation

/s/, /z/ and /ɪz/

a 🔊 Listen and write the verbs in the lists.

/s/	/z/	/ɪz/
stops	_goes_	_watches_
....	....	....
....	....	....
	....	

| ~~goes~~ | ~~watches~~ | ~~stops~~ | reads | studies |
| works | learns | gives | finishes | likes |

b 🔊 Listen again and repeat.

4 Speak

a Work with a partner. Ask the questions in Exercise 2g and use short answers.

A: *Does J.K. Rowling live in America?*
B: *No, she doesn't.*

b Make questions. Then ask your partner.

1 Do you watch   a Harry Potter books?
2 Do you study   b volleyball?
3 Do you play   c French at school?
4 Do you read   d pop music?
5 Do you listen to   e cartoons on TV?

c Make sentences about your partner. Tell other students.

(Davide) doesn't watch cartoons on TV. He studies French at school. He ...

5 Vocabulary

Family

a Write the words from the box in the spaces. Check with the article on page 26.

> aunt mother father uncle

Harry Potter's _____ and _____ are dead. He lives with his _____ and _____ .

b 🔊 Look at Sally's family tree. Write the words from the box in the spaces. Then listen to Sally and check your answers.

> cousin mother father
> ~~uncle~~ aunt ~~grandfather~~
> brother sister grandmother

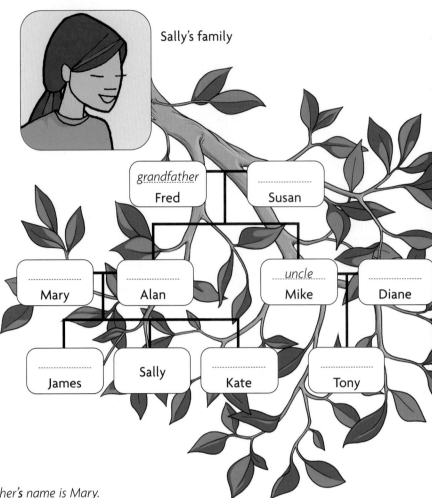

Sally's family

grandfather
Fred

_____
Susan

_____
Mary

_____
Alan

uncle
Mike

_____
Diane

_____
James

Sally

Kate

_____
Tony

6 Grammar

Possessive *'s*

a Look at the examples.

My father's name is Alan, and my mother's name is Mary.
My grandmother and grandfather are my father's parents.

b Look at the pictures and write the correct words with *'s*.

1 *Peter's book.* _____

2 _____

3 _____

My father

My sister

My brother

4 _____

5 _____

6 _____

Possessive adjectives

c Look at the examples.

Writing is her hobby and her work.   He lives with his aunt and uncle.   He doesn't like their son Dudley.

d Complete the table.

Singular	I	you	she **her**	he	it ....
Plural	we **our**	you	they		

e Write words from Exercise 6d in the spaces.

1 Hi! _____My_____ name's Jenny. Nice to meet you. What's _____ name?

2 My brother really likes music. _____ favourite singer's Robbie Williams.

3 I've got two sisters. _____ names are Sally and Joanna.

4 Amy's American. She's here in England with _____ family.

5 We live in London now, but we don't really like _____ house.

6 Do you and your sister like _____ new house?

7 Speak

a Work with a partner. Look at Sally's family tree on page 28. Ask and answer questions about her family.

A: *Who's Alan?*
B: *He's Sally's father.*

B: *Is Tony Sally's brother?*
A: *No, he isn't. He's her cousin.*

b Draw your family tree. Write *father, mother, grandfather*, but not their names!

c Work with a partner. Swap your family trees and fill in the names.

My mother's name is Gabriela and my father's name is Manuel. My sister's name is ....

8 Listen

a Match the verbs with the pictures. Write a–f in the boxes.

a go for a walk   c have a fight   e work in a factory
b go shopping   d work in a shop   f go to the cinema

b 🔊 Listen to Mark's questions. Then look at the pictures and write 1–6 to show the correct order.

........5........ ....

Culture in mind

9 Read

a Read about two different British families. Where is each family from?

British families

1 The Ashraf family live in Manchester, in the north of England. Kashif and his wife Sabeen have four children. Kashif is British but Sabeen comes from Pakistan. They live with Kashif's mother and father. Two of his cousins live in the same road.

The family have a small shop. It sells newspapers, sweets and drinks. Kashif and his cousins work in the shop.

Sabeen works at home. She looks after the house, the children and her parents-in-law.

2 This is Craig Carter. He's 14. He has a father, a mother and a brother (he's 16), and they all live in a house in a city called Canterbury in the south of England. At the back of their house they have a garden.

Craig's family has a car, a computer, a colour TV and video, a washing machine, a dishwasher and a cat.

His dad works with computers. His mum works part time at a hospital. She's a nurse.

b Complete the missing information in the table.

	City	Number of children	Mother's job	Father's job
The Ashraf family			*works at home*	
The Carter family				

c Are families different in different parts of your country?

10 Write

a Read Jenny's web page about her family. Write names under the pictures.

Jenny Groves

Hi. I'm Jenny Groves. I'm 15, and I live in Bristol. I love it – it's a fantastic city!

This is my sister Annie – she's 13. We go shopping together at the weekends. My brother Andy's 18. He works in a shop in town. He's OK, but we have fights sometimes.

This is my father – his name's Mark, he's 44, and he's a teacher. My mother's name is Susan – she's 44, too, and she works in a bank.

My grandparents' names are Arthur and Lynne. They're great! They live in Reading, near London.

1 _____ *Jenny* _____

Internet zone

b Write a paragraph about your family. Use Jenny's web page to help you.

Module 1 Check your progress

1 Grammar

a) Write the words in the correct order.

1 am / I / an / town / old / from / Italy / in
   I am from an old town in Italy .

2 are / friends / great / singers / My
   _____ .

3 fantastic / London / a / city / is
   _____ .

4 really / are / restaurants / Polish / good
   _____ .

[ ] 3

b) Write the words from the box in the spaces.

| ~~do~~ | are | does | doesn't | don't | isn't |
| is | aren't | | | | |

1 ____*Do*____ you play football?
2 My brother _____ like U2.
3 _____ you from Turkey?
4 She _____ Swiss, she's Italian.
5 _____ your sister like music?
6 _____ Julia Roberts Australian?
7 They _____ British, they're American!
8 My mother and father _____
   like pop music!

[ ] 7

c) Write a word from the box in the spaces.

| my | ~~his~~ | her | our | your | their |

1 Antonio's father is Canadian but ____*his*____
   mother is Italian.
2 We live in Rochester now, but my brother and
   I don't like _____ new school.
3 A: Hello, _____ name's Christine. What's
      _____ name?
   B: Hi, I'm Caroline.
4 Karen's got a really nice sister. _____
   name's Patricia.
5 Jackie and Nigel live in Canterbury
   now, but _____ sons are still in
   London.

[ ] 5

d) Write the question words from the box in the spaces.

| ~~What~~ | Why | Where | Who | How |

1 A: ____*What*____ is this?
   B: It's a Brazilian flag.
2 A: _____ old is your brother?
   B: He's 14.
3 A: _____ is your English teacher?
   B: Mrs Welch.
4 A: _____ is your little sister excited?
   B: Because it's her birthday party today.
5 A: _____ do you come from?
   B: I'm from Poland.

[ ] 4

e) Write the correct words in the spaces.

1 He ____*studies*____ Polish at school. (study)
2 She _____ English and Italian. (speak)
3 We _____ TV at the weekend. (watch)
4 He _____ his homework before tea. (finish)
5 My friend _____ to jazz dance classes. (go)
6 They _____ to music in their room. (listen)

[ ] 5

2 Vocabulary

a) Write the countries.

1 A _U_ _S_ _T_ _R_ _A_ _L_ _I_ _A_
2 B ___ ___ ___ ___ ___ M
3 B ___ ___ ___ ___ ___ N
4 I ___ ___ ___ Y
5 P ___ ___ ___ ___ D
6 T ___ ___ ___ ___ Y
7 J ___ ___ ___ N
8 C ___ ___ ___ ___ A

[ ] 7

b) Write the nationalities for people from the countries in Exercise 2a.

1 *Australian* _____
2 _____
3 _____
4 _____
5 _____
6 _____
7 _____
8 _____

[ ] 7

(c) Write the plurals.

1   one man: two   _men_
2   one singer: six ....
3   one person: seven ....
4   one woman: five ....
5   one teacher: three ....   ☐ 4

(d) Match the opposites.

1   big   a   expensive
2   interesting   b   bad
3   good   c   terrible
4   cheap   d   new
5   old   e   boring
6   fantastic   f   small   ☐ 5

(e) Write the words from the box in three lists.

pen   cassette   twenty-one   ~~son~~   parents
aunt   notebook   father   book   chair
fourteen   ~~fifty~~   daughter   cousin   pencil
~~desk~~   uncle   thirteen   seventy   door
eight   mother   two   thirty

In the classroom

........._desk_.........   ....
....
....
....

Family

........._son_.........   ....
....
....
....

Numbers

........._fifty_.........   ....
....
....
....   ☐ 21

3 Everyday English

Complete the dialogues with the expressions in the box.

Guess what   I don't understand
~~No problem~~   that's right
Let's go together

1   Jade: I don't know the answer.
    Alan: ¹ _No problem._ , Jade! I can help you.

2   Sue: James, a good film is on at the cinema tonight.
    James: Great. ² ....

3   Matt: You're Swiss, aren't you?
    Urli: Yes, ³ .... I'm from Zurich.

4   Man: Do you understand this sign?
    Alan: I'm sorry. ⁴ .... Russian.

5   Phil: Hey, Josh. ⁵ .... ? U2 are on TV.
    Josh: Great! Let's watch them!   ☐ 4

How did you do?

Tick (✓) a box for each section.

Total score ☐ 72	☺ Very good	☹ OK	☹ Not very good
Grammar	19 – 24	13 – 18	less than 13
Vocabulary	35 – 44	20 – 34	less than 20
Everyday English	3 – 4	2	less than 2

Module 2
People and places

YOU WILL LEARN ABOUT ...

- Famous English cities ...... 2 ......
- Chimpanzees and humans ....
- Food around the world ....
- Two different teenagers ....
- British teenagers and TV ....

⁕ Can you match each photo with a topic?

YOU WILL LEARN HOW TO ...

Speak
- Give directions
- Talk about your family and things you've got
- Give personal information
- Talk about food you like and don't like
- Order food in a restaurant
- Talk about how often you do things
- Interview a partner about television they watch
- Talk about your daily routine

Write
- A text about your town/city
- Short descriptions of people
- A letter to a host family
- A paragraph about TV you watch

Read
- A web page about London
- A text about humans and chimpanzees
- A magazine article about pets in the UK
- An article about strange food in different countries
- An article about different lives in Australia and America
- A text about someone watching TV

Listen
- People giving directions
- Descriptions of people
- A dialogue in a restaurant
- An interview about watching TV

Use grammar

Can you match the names of the grammar points with the examples?

there's / there are   **Buy** a travel card and **take** the tube.

Positive imperatives   **I'd like** some apples, please.

Prepositions of place   The station is **opposite** the park.

have / has got   **There are** over 300 museums in London.

Countable/Uncountable nouns   **An** apple and **some** sugar.

this, that, these, those   Judy **never** goes to school.

I'd like / Would you like ...?   **I've got** three sisters.

Present simple / adverbs of frequency   **These** are your chips.

Use vocabulary

Can you think of two more examples for each topic?

Places in towns	Parts of the body	Food	Days of the week	TV programmes
post office	head	strawberries	Monday	documentaries
newsagent	leg	cheese	Saturday	the news
....	....	....	....	....
....	....	....	....	....

5 Where's the café?

* *there's / there are*
* Positive imperatives
* Prepositions of place
* Vocabulary: places in towns; numbers 100 +

1 Read and listen

🔊 Read the web page and match the pictures and the paragraphs. Write a–f in the boxes. Then read the web page again and listen.

f

A great trip to **London!**

Is there a lot to do in London? Yes, there is! Look at these six great ideas for a fantastic day out.

1 Buy a travel card and take the Underground (called the Tube). There's a big underground train system in London, with 12 train lines. One of the Underground lines is about 140 years old! b

2 Take a 30 minute flight in the London Eye and see the wonderful sights of London from 130 metres in the air! ☐

3 Go on a fantastic river boat tour on the Thames. There are tours every day. ☐

4 Do you want to buy cheap, fashionable clothes? Try one of the fantastic street markets! There's a great market for young people in Camden. ☐

5 Are there any interesting museums? Yes, there are! There are over 300 museums in London. Visit the Natural History Museum, for example. There's a great dinosaur collection there! ☐

6 Do you like music? Go to a concert! There are different concerts every day with singers and bands from around the world. ☐

a

b  UNDERGROUND

c

d

e

36 Module 2

2 Vocabulary

Numbers 100 +

🔊 Listen and repeat the numbers.

120	a hundred and twenty	500	five hundred
150	a hundred and fifty	1,000	a thousand
200	two hundred	2,000	two thousand
300	three hundred		

3 Pronunciation

🔊 /ð/ and /θ/

Listen and repeat.

/ð/		/θ/	
there	the	thousand	think
mother	father	thirty	three

4 Grammar

there's / there are

a Look at the examples. Then complete the rule and the table.

There are over 300 museums in London.
There's a great dinosaur collection.
Is there a lot to do in London?
Are there any interesting museums?

	Singular nouns	Plural nouns
Statements	There's a market.	There .... shops.
Negatives	There **isn't a** museum.	There **aren't any** concerts.
Questions	Is there **a** market?	.... there **any** shops?
Short answers	Yes, there .... No, there **isn't**.	Yes, there .... No, there ....

....

Rule: *There* .... *a/an* + singular nouns. *There* ....
+ plural nouns. Use *any* in .... and negative sentences with
plural nouns.

....

b Complete the sentences. Use *There's / There isn't* or *There are / There aren't any*.

1 _____*There's*_____ a big park in London called 'Hyde Park'. (✓)

2 __*There aren't any*__ good shops in my street. (✗)

3 .... cheap clothes in Camden Market. (✓)

4 .... a museum in my town. (✗)

5 .... a concert on Friday. (✓)

6 .... singers in this classroom. (✗)

7 .... good restaurants here. (✗)

5 Vocabulary
Places in towns

a 🔊 Write the names of the places under the pictures. Then listen, check and repeat.

bank   park   bookshop   newsagent   chemist   post office   ~~library~~   railway station   supermarket

1 _____library_____

2 _____

3 _____

4 _____

5 _____

6 _____

7 _____

8 _____

9 _____

b Work with a partner. Make questions about your town or city.

A: *Is there a museum in your town?*
B: *Yes, there is. Are there any good bookshops in your town?*

c Where do you do these things?

You buy shampoo in a chemist or supermarket.

buy shampoo	send a parcel
catch a train	buy stamps
change money	buy milk
play football	buy a magazine

6 Grammar
Positive imperatives

a Look at the examples and the rule.

Go to a concert!
*Buy a travel card and **take** the tube.*

> **Rule:** Use the base form of the verb (infinitive without *to*).

b Match the two parts of the sentences.

1 Change
2 Buy
3 Watch
4 Listen
5 Pay
6 Sit

a to your teacher.
b stamps here.
c for travel cards here.
d down, please.
e this film, it's great!
f money here.

c Listen to your teacher's instructions.

7 Listen, read and speak

Directions

a 🔊 Two people ask for directions. Listen and read. Then write the names of the places on the map.

Tourist 1: Excuse me, where's the railway station?

Man: It's in the High Street, opposite the park.

Tourist 1: And is there a post office near here?

Man: Yes, there is. Go down the High Street and turn left. There's a post office on Smith Street, next to Clare's café.

Tourist 1: Thank you.

Man: You're welcome.

Tourist 2: Excuse me, is there a bank near here?

Woman: Yes, there is. Turn right into Rich Way. It's next to the supermarket.

Tourist 2: Thank you.

b Look at the map. Say where the things are.

The newsagent's is next to the bookshop.

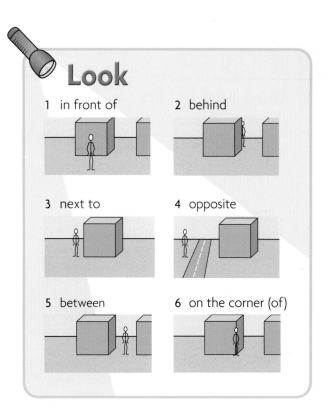

Look

1 in front of

2 behind

3 next to

4 opposite

5 between

6 on the corner (of)

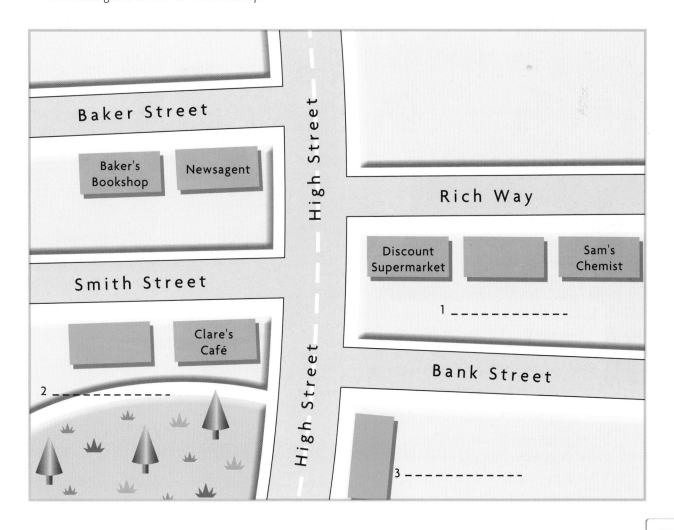

I have no idea!

8 Read and listen

a 🔊 Look at the photo story. Who does something stupid? What does he or she do? Read and listen to check your answers.

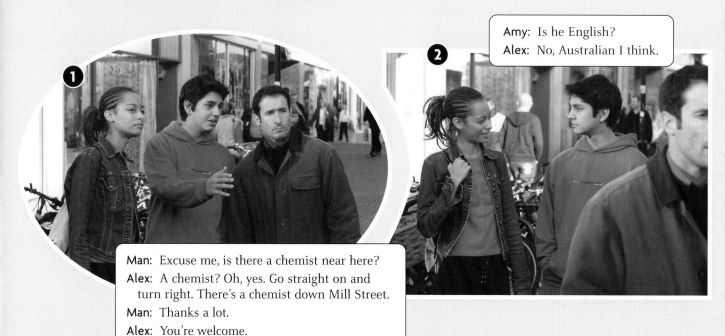

2

Amy: Is he English?
Alex: No, Australian I think.

1

Man: Excuse me, is there a chemist near here?
Alex: A chemist? Oh, yes. Go straight on and turn right. There's a chemist down Mill Street.
Man: Thanks a lot.
Alex: You're welcome.

Next day at school ...

3

Amy: Wait a minute, Alex. Mill Street? Are you sure there's a chemist down there?
Alex: I have no idea!
Amy: Oh, Alex. What a stupid thing to do!

4

Man: Good morning, I'm Mr Thomas. I'm your new Biology teacher.
Alex: Oh no. I think I'm in trouble!

b Answer the questions.

1 What does the man want to know?
2 Does Alex give him the right answer?
3 What does Amy think about Alex?
4 What happens the next day at school?

9 Everyday English

a Find the expressions in the photo story. Who says them? How do you say them in your language?

1 You're welcome.
2 Wait a minute.
3 Are you sure?
4 I have no idea.

b Read the dialogues. Fill in the spaces with the words in Exercise 9a.

1 Mrs Simmons: Thank you very much, Cathy.

   Cathy: ....

2 Thomas: The film starts in ten minutes! Come on!

   Ken: .... !
   Where are my shoes?

3 Marina: Is there a café in this street?

   Franco: ....
   Let's ask in the shop over there.

4 Nick: The library isn't in this street.

   Anne: .... ?
   I think it's near the bank.

10 Write

a Read Rob's text about Cambridge. Match topics 1–3 with the paragraphs. Write A, B and C in the boxes.

1 The shops and restaurants ☐

2 Things to see in the city ☐

3 Rob's opinion of Cambridge ☐

A I'm from Cambridge. It's a beautiful city with a very old university. There are fantastic old buildings in the city centre, and there's a very big park called 'Midsummer Common'. There's also a big university library, and a museum called 'The Fitzwilliam Museum'.

B There are interesting shops, but there aren't any really big street markets. London is only one hour by train, so I go shopping in London too. There are good cafés in Cambridge. My favourite café is Italian. I like Italian coffee and food a lot!

C Cambridge is great. I really like it here!

Rob

b Write a short text about your town or city. Use Rob's text to help you.

6 They've got brown eyes

* has / have got
* why ... ? because ...
* Vocabulary: colours; parts of the body

1 Read and listen

a Read the text. Who is Sally? Who is Paula? Write 'Sally' or 'Paula' under the pictures.

b 🔊 Now read the text again and listen. Mark the statements *T* (true) or *F* (false).

1 Sally and Paula have got big families. ☐
2 Paula's got three sisters. ☐
3 Sally doesn't like her sisters. ☐
4 People and chimpanzees have very different DNA. ☐

Sally or Paula?

She's four years old. She's intelligent, and she's got brown hair and brown eyes. She's got a small nose and a big smile. She's got four fingers and a thumb on her hand. She lives with her family. She hasn't got a big family, she's got two sisters. She likes people and she loves her sisters and her friends. She loves chocolate and she likes bananas, too! Paula and Sally are similar, but Paula's a little girl, and Sally's a chimpanzee!

A little girl

NAME: _____

A chimpanzee

How are Sally and Paula different? Chimpanzees live in forests and people live in towns and cities. People drive cars, write books, play music, and use computers. But of course chimpanzees don't do these things.

So why are chimpanzees and people similar? The answer is because they've got similar DNA. The DNA of people and chimpanzees is 98% the same. Sally and Paula look very different, but when we study the DNA, we see that they aren't very different at all.

NAME: _____

2 Grammar

why ...? because ...

a Look at the text on page 42 again. Then answer the question.

Why are chimpanzees and people similar?   *Because* they've got similar DNA.

Why is Sally happy when she gets chocolate? _____ .

has / have got

b Look at the examples. Then complete the table.

She's got four fingers and a thumb on her hand.   *She hasn't got* a big family.   *They've got* similar DNA.

Positive	Negative	Question	Short answer
I/you/we/they**'ve (have) got.**	I/you/we/they .... (have not) got.	**Have** I/you/we/they **got?**	Yes, I/you/we/they .... No, I/you/we/they .... **(have not).**
He/she/it**'s (has) got.**	He/she/it **hasn't** (has not) got.	.... he/she/it **got?**	Yes, he/she/it .... No, he/she/it ....**(has not).**

c Make true sentences about you and your family. Use the correct form of *have got*.

1   I _____ a big family.
2   My family _____ a big house.
3   My best friend _____ brother.
4   I _____ a bicycle.
5   I _____ a computer.
6   I _____ a sister.

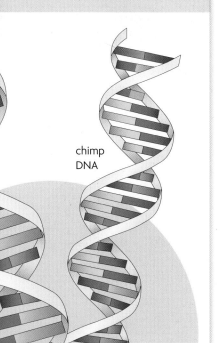

chimp
DNA

3 Pronunciation

/v/ they've

a 🔊 Listen and repeat.

1	they've	4	I've	7	verb
2	we've	5	very	8	video
3	you've	6	five	9	volleyball

b 🔊 Say the sentences. Then listen, check and repeat.

1   We've got five very big videos.
2   You've got the wrong verb.
3   I've got volleyball practice today.

4 Speak

Work with a partner. Ask and answer questions with *have got*.

A: *Have you got a big family?*
B: *No, I haven't. Have you got ... ?*

DNA

5 Vocabulary

Colours

(a) 🔊 Listen and repeat.

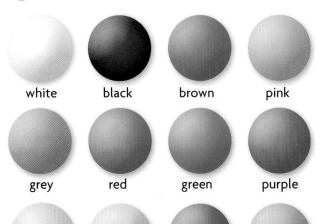

white   black   brown   pink

grey   red   green   purple

beige   yellow   blue   orange

(b) Find things in your classroom and say the colours.

There's a red pen.

Parts of the body

(c) 🔊 Write the words from the box in the spaces. Then listen, check and repeat.

| hand |
| leg |
| finger |
| arm |
| foot |
| thumb |
| mouth |
| ear |
| nose |
| face |
| hair |
| eye |

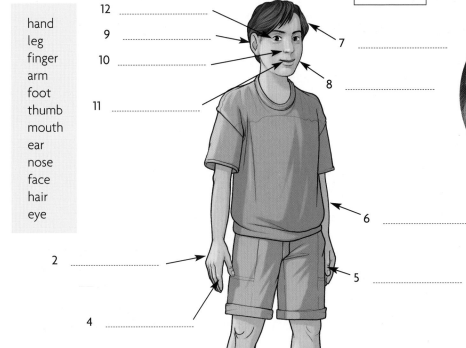

12 ....
9 ....
10 ....
11 ....
7 ....
8 ....
6 ....
2 ....
5 ....
4 ....
1 ....
3 ....

Describing people

(d) 🔊 Write the words in the box in the correct lists. Then listen, check and repeat.

~~blonde~~   ~~brown~~ (x2)   short   red   blue
grey (x2)   ~~straight~~   curly   fair   wavy
medium-length   green   black   long

Hair colour	Hair style	Eye colour
blonde	*straight*	*brown*

(e) Use the words in the box to describe the people in the pictures.

A: *Brad Pitt's got blue eyes.*
B: *Julia Roberts has got long, curly hair and ...*

Brad Pitt

Halle Berry

Jennifer Aniston

Julia Roberts

6 Listen and speak

Describing people

a 🔊 Listen to descriptions of two of the people in the pictures. Tick (✓) the pictures of the people they describe.

①  ②  ③  ④

b Find a picture of a person in *English In Mind Starter*. Don't show your partner. Describe the person. Your partner says who it is.

A: *He's good-looking. He's got short dark hair and brown eyes. He's got a nice smile.*
B: *Is it ... ?*

Giving personal information

c 🔊 Amy wants to join a video club. Listen and write her information on the form.

Video Store
Mill Road

MEMBERSHIP FORM

First name: _____ *Amy* _____
Surname: _____
Age: _____
Address: _____
_____ Cambridge
Telephone: _____ Mobile: _____

d Put the words in order to make questions.

1 old / you / are / How   *How old are you?* ?
2 name / first / your / What's _____ ?
3 spell / How / you / do / please / that
_____ ?
4 your / What's / address _____ ?
5 you / that / Can / repeat / please
_____ ?
6 number / please / telephone / your / What's
_____ ?

e Work with a partner.
Ask and answer questions from Exercise 6d.

What's your first name?
How do you spell that, please?

Culture in mind

7 Read

a Read the magazine article. What do men and women usually buy for their pets? Write *M* (men) or *W* (women) in the boxes next to the pictures.

1 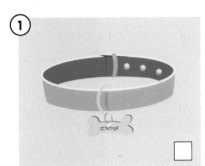 ☐

2 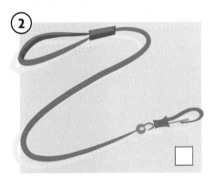 ☐

3 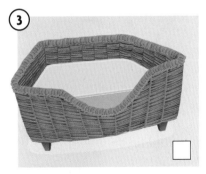 ☐

4  ☐

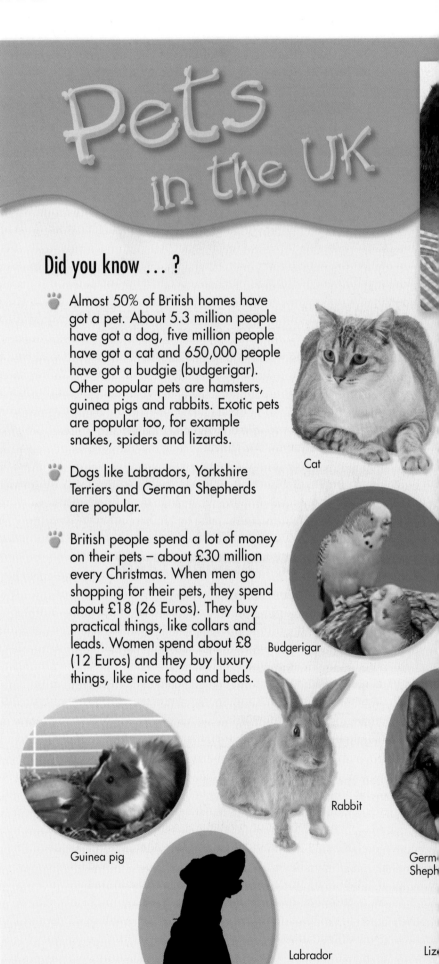

Pets in the UK

Did you know … ?

🐾 Almost 50% of British homes have got a pet. About 5.3 million people have got a dog, five million people have got a cat and 650,000 people have got a budgie (budgerigar). Other popular pets are hamsters, guinea pigs and rabbits. Exotic pets are popular too, for example snakes, spiders and lizards.

🐾 Dogs like Labradors, Yorkshire Terriers and German Shepherds are popular.

🐾 British people spend a lot of money on their pets – about £30 million every Christmas. When men go shopping for their pets, they spend about £18 (26 Euros). They buy practical things, like collars and leads. Women spend about £8 (12 Euros) and they buy luxury things, like nice food and beds.

Cat

Budgerigar

Guinea pig

Rabbit

Germ Sheph

Labrador

Liz

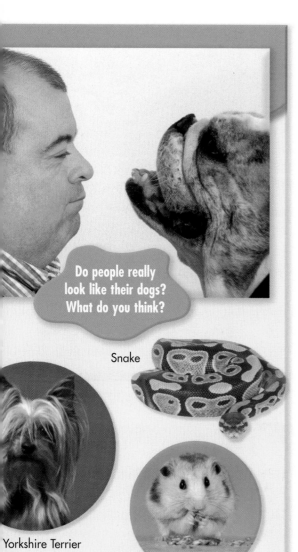

Do people really look like their dogs? What do you think?

Snake

Yorkshire Terrier

Hamster

🐾 Pets are expensive. Dogs and cats break about £1 million of electrical equipment (stereos, TVs and DVD players) every year in their owners' houses.

🐾 People like to name their pets after famous people: Becks (after David Beckham), Britney (after Britney Spears), Batman and Homer (after Homer Simpson) are popular names for cats and dogs. Some cats are called Hobbit and Bilbo Baggins after 'Lord of the Rings' characters.

Spider

(b) Read the text again and answer the questions.

1 How many British homes have a pet?
2 How many people have got budgies?
3 What exotic pets are popular in the UK?
4 How much money do British people spend on their pets at Christmas?
5 What kinds of things do pets break in their homes?
6 Give some examples of popular names for British people's pets.

(c) What kinds of pets are popular in your country?

8 Write

(a) Read Anna's descriptions of her brother and her best friend. Match the descriptions with the pictures. Write the numbers in the boxes.

1 My brother's name's Matt, and he's 15. He wears glasses and he's got brown eyes and short brown hair. He really likes music. His favourite band is Red Hot Chilli Peppers.

2 My best friend's name's Davide and he's 14. He's from France but he lives in London. He's good-looking and he's got short fair hair and green eyes. He likes sports and he plays tennis and football.

(b) Write two short descriptions of your friends or family. Use Anna's texts to help you.

7 This is delicious!

* *I'd like / Would you like ... ?*
* Countable and uncountable nouns
* *this / that / these / those*
* Vocabulary: food

1 Read and listen

a Look at the pictures. Where do some people eat these things?
Match the pictures with the countries. Write a–f in the boxes.

a Brazil **b** Britain **c** France **d** Mexico **e** the USA **f** Australia

1

rattlesnake

2
grasshopper

3

chips

4

alligator

5

snails

6

kangaroo

b Read the article and listen. Check your answers to Exercise 1a.

Would you like our Special?

You are in the USA and you are hungry, so you go into a restaurant. Your waiter says, 'Would you like our special today? It's rattlesnake.' What do you say?

'Rattlesnake? Yes, why not?' Or 'Rattlesnake? That's disgusting. No thank you. I'd like a burger please.'

Perhaps you think rattlesnake is a really strange thing to eat.

But in the USA some people eat it and they think it's delicious.

All around the world people eat things that perhaps you think are strange. In Australia, kangaroo meat is very popular, and some people in Brazil eat alligator steaks. In France, some people love snails, and in Mexico, some people really like grasshoppers. Of course, people who eat grasshoppers don't

think they're strange. In fact, grasshoppers are good for you, but burgers and chips are not! In Britain, some people eat their chips with vinegar, but in Holland, they eat chips with mayonnaise.

So, when you eat a meal, stop and think. Perhaps people from other countries think that your food is really strange!

2 Vocabulary

Food

a 🔊 Look at the food in the pictures and write the words in the spaces. Then listen, check, and repeat.

| tomatoes | eggs | bread | strawberries |
| cheese | chicken | onions | apples | bananas |

b Tell your partner which things you like and which you don't like.

A: *I like bananas.*

B: *Oh, I don't like them, but I love apples.*

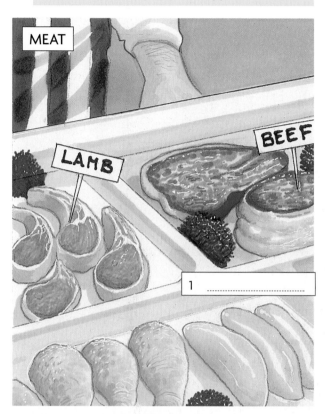

MEAT

LAMB

BEEF

1 ....

FRUIT

2 ....

3 ....

4 ....

ORANGES

GRAPES

VEGETABLES   6 ....

LETTUCE

5 ....

CARROTS

POTATOES

GROCERIES

7 ....   8 ....

WHOLEMEAL

SUGAR

RICE

9 ....

3 Grammar

Countable and uncountable nouns

a Look at the table and the pictures on page 49. Write the words in the box in the spaces.

tomato ~~apple~~ egg bread ~~salt~~
strawberry orange chicken sugar
onion ~~cheese~~ beef ~~banana~~ rice

Countable	Uncountable
an apple	*some salt*
a banana	*some cheese*

b Look at the table in Exercise 3a and complete the rule.

> **Rule:** With singular countable nouns, we use *a* or ....
> With uncountable nouns, we use ....
> With plural countable nouns, we use *some*.

this/that/these/those

This is my water.

That is our bus.

These are your chips.

Those are her parents.

c Look at the pictures and fill in the spaces with *this*, *that*, *these* and *those*.

① .... are his sandwiches.

② Is .... my bag?

③ .... aren't her shoes.

④ I think .... is your ice cream.

d Listen to the dialogue. What does the man want to buy?

Woman: Good morning. Can I help you?

Man: Yes, I'd like some apples, please. Two kilos. And some of those strawberries, too. I'd like a kilo I think, please.

Woman: Would you like anything else?

Man: Yes, please. I'd like some salad ... er, that lettuce looks nice. Erm ... and I'd like a kilo of onions, five kilos of potatoes and ...

Woman: Would you like some tomatoes, too? These are lovely.

Man: No, thanks – I don't like tomatoes!

e Write words in the spaces to make questions and answers.

1 A: *Would you .... anything else?*

2 B: *Yes, ... I .... some salad.*

3 A: *............................ some tomatoes, too?*

4 B: *No, ...*

4 Pronunciation

/w/ would

 Listen and repeat.

1 Would you like a sandwich?

2 Are you the new waiter?

3 What do you want to eat?

4 Where in the world are you from?

5 Listen and speak

a Look at the menu. Listen and tick (✓) the things that the people order.

Lunchtime menu

STARTERS

Soup of the day
Mushroom pâté and toast
Goat's cheese salad ✓

MAIN COURSES

Chicken with honey and mustard
Vegetable lasagne
Roast lamb

* All our main courses come with chips or potatoes and a selection of vegetables or salad

DESSERTS

Fresh fruit salad
Chocolate mousse
Apple pie

DRINKS

Cola
Fresh fruit juice
Lemonade
Tea
Coffee

b Work in small groups. Role play dialogues in a restaurant. Take turns to be the waiter and the customer. Use the phrases in the box to help you.

> Are you ready to order?
> Would you like chips or potatoes?
> What would you like to drink?

I'm really hungry!

6 Read and listen

a What fast food do Amy and Lucy eat? Read, listen and check your answer.

1

Amy: I'm really hungry. I'd like a hamburger.
Lucy: Really?

2

Amy: What's wrong?
Lucy: Well, fast food's really bad for you.
Amy: One little burger's no problem!
Lucy: Do you think so?
Amy: I don't think so, Lucy, I *know*.

3

Lucy: Oh, wow! This is delicious.

4

Amy: But listen, Lucy. Tomorrow ...
Lucy: Yeah, I know. Healthy food!

b Put these sentences into the correct order.

1 Amy buys a hamburger. ☐
2 Amy says one burger is OK. ☐
3 They really like the hamburgers. ☐
4 Amy is very hungry. a
5 Lucy thinks fast food is not a good idea. ☐

7 Everyday English

(a) Find the expressions in the story. Who says them? How do you say them in your language?

1 I'm really hungry.
2 Really?
3 What's wrong?
4 Do you think so?

(b) Complete the dialogues with the expressions 1–4 in Exercise 7a.

1 Angela: There are about 15,000 restaurants in New York.
   Barbara: 15,000? _____ ?
   Angela: Yes, it's true. I've got a book about it, look!

2 Claire: Would you like a sandwich?
   Alex: Oh, yes, please. _____ !

3 Fredek: Sugar in your tea is bad for you.
   Basia: _____ ? I think it's OK.

4 Meral: I just hate it!
   Selim: Hey, Meral. _____ ?
   Meral: I don't like my hair. I want to change it.

8 Write

(a) You are going to Britain next month to stay with an English family. Read the letter they send you. Where do they live? What do they want to know?

Dear _____

We're very happy you want to stay with us in England next month. We'd like to learn all about what you like before you arrive. Please write to us and tell us all about you! What food do you like? Is there any food you don't like? What's your favourite food?

Also, please tell us what you'd like to do here in London!

Best wishes and see you soon.

Mr and Mrs Johnson

P.S. This is a photo of us with our dog, Ruff. Please send us a photo of you!

(b) Write your reply to Mr and Mrs Johnson. Start like this:

Dear Mr and Mrs Johnson,

Thank you for your letter and the photo!
Here's a photo of me and my family.

8 I sometimes watch soaps

❋ Present simple with adverbs of frequency
❋ Vocabulary: days of the week, TV programmes, telling the time

1 Read and listen

a Look at the pictures of Joshua and Judy. Which activities do you think they do? Put a tick (✓) or a cross (✗) in the correct places. Then read the article to check your ideas.

	Joshua	Judy
1 watches TV	✗	
2 lives on a farm		
3 goes to school		
4 goes shopping		
5 listens to the radio		

b 🔊 Read the article again and listen. Answer the questions.

1 Where is Joshua from? Where is Judy from?
2 Does Joshua watch TV? Why / Why not?
3 Does Judy go to school? Why / Why not?
4 What does Judy do in the morning and in the evening?

Different lives

Judy

lives on a farm in Australia, 600 kilometres from the nearest town. Judy never goes to school because she learns from home.

Three times a week, she listens to lessons on the radio. She often watches school programmes on television. 'There are so many things to do on the farm,' says Judy. 'I help my father every morning, but I sometimes watch TV in the evenings. I like soaps, for example.'

Judy sometimes talks to her teacher on the radio, but she hardly ever sees him. He comes to her house only once a year to help her with her school work.

Joshua

lives on a farm in Pennsylvania, USA. Joshua's family are Amish. The Amish people live in a very different way from other people in the United States. For example, they always wear very simple traditional clothes. They never watch TV because they do not have electricity and they hardly ever play musical instruments.

Five days a week, Joshua goes to a school for Amish children. He sometimes goes into the city with his parents to do the shopping. When they go to the city, they use a horse and buggy, because the Amish people do not have cars.

2 Vocabulary

The days of the week

🔊 Listen and repeat.

Monday
Tuesday
Wednesday
Thursday
Friday
Saturday
Sunday

3 Grammar

Adverbs of frequency

100%	always
	usually
	often
	sometimes
	hardly ever
0%	never

a Complete the sentences about Joshua and Judy with words from the table.

1 Judy ___never___ goes to school.
2 Joshua _____ watches TV.
3 Judy _____ helps her father in the morning.
4 Joshua _____ goes shopping with his parents.
5 Judy _____watches school TV programmes.
6 The teacher_____ comes to Judy's house.
7 Amish clothes are _____ traditional.

b Complete the rule. Write *before* or *after* in the spaces.

> **Rule:** Adverbs of frequency usually come _____ the verb *be*, but _____ other verbs.

c You can also talk about frequency like this.

every	day week morning month year	
once twice three times five days	a	day week month year

*I help my father **every morning**.*
***Five days a week**, Joshua goes to a special school for Amish children.*
*Judy's teacher comes to her house only **once a year**.*

d 🔊 Complete the sentences with words from Exercise 3c. Then listen and check.

1 My mum checks her email at 08.00 and 20.00.
   _My mum checks her email twice a day_____ .
2 Tom eats fish on Tuesday and Friday.
   _____ _a week_ .
3 Susan goes shopping on Monday, Wednesday and Saturday.
   _____ .
4 Harry plays football on Saturday.
   _____ .

4 Speak

Work with a partner. Tell him/her about you. Use words from the box.

> play football   go swimming   watch TV   go shopping
> do homework   go to the cinema   eat bananas   check email
> wear black   ...... (your ideas)

A: *I check my email once a day.*
B: *I never eat bananas because I don't like them.*

5 Vocabulary

TV programmes

a How many TV channels are there in your country? Which do you like? Are there interesting TV programmes for teenagers in your country?

b Look at the pictures, listen and repeat the names. Then think of an example for each type from your country.

6 Pronunciation

Compound nouns

a Listen. Is the stress on the first word, or on the second word?

chat shows   game shows
sports programmes   soap operas

b Listen again and repeat.

1

soap operas

2

documentaries

3

sports programmes

4

game shows

5

the news

6

chat shows

7

comedies

8

cartoons

7 Listen and speak

a 🔊 Listen to the two interviews. Complete the table with information about how often the two people watch TV.

How often?	Interview 1	Interview 2	Me	My partner
TV	*3 times a week*	*5 or 6 days a week*		
chat shows				
sports programmes	*usually*			
comedies				
documentaries				
the news				
soap operas				
game shows				
cartoons				

b What do you watch? Complete the *Me* column in Exercise 7a.

c Work with a partner. Ask and answer questions to complete the *My partner* column.

A: *Do you like chat shows?*
B: *Yes, I do.*
A: *How often do you watch them?*

8 Vocabulary

What's the time?

a 🔊 Listen. Write the numbers in the boxes. Then listen again and repeat.

b 🔊 Listen to these times. Then listen again and repeat.

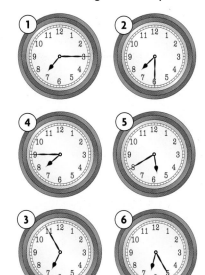

9 Speak

Look at the table. Write the times for you under *Me*.

Work with a partner. Ask and answer questions and write the times under My Partner.

A: *What time do you usually get up in the morning?*
B: *At half past six. What time do you get up?*
A: *I usually get up at seven o'clock.*

	Me	My Partner
get up in the morning		*6.30*
have breakfast		
arrive at school		
have lunch		
do your homework		
have dinner		

c 🔊 Listen to the four conversations. Write the times you hear.

1 .... 2 .... 3 .... 4 ....

Culture in mind

10 Read and listen

a Look at the pictures of Jane and Mark. What kinds of TV programmes do they like, do you think? Read the profile of Jane and complete the information in the table in Exercise 10b.

What British teenagers watch

Jane Taylor

Jane is 16. She lives near Macclesfield, in Cheshire in the north of England. Here is what she says about watching TV.

'I don't watch a lot of TV – only about five or six hours a week, I think. My favourite programme is a soap opera; it's called 'EastEnders', and I watch it every week. Monday is the day I watch TV most, because there are other soap operas as well! I always watch soap operas. I sometimes watch chat shows and films, and I also watch comedy programmes and documentaries. I never watch sports programmes, or cartoons! And I don't like game shows or news programmes very much, so I hardly ever watch them.'

Macclesfield

London

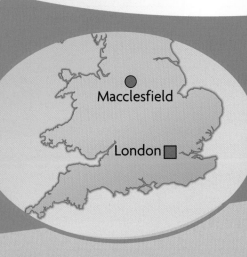

Mark Fields

b 🔊 Now listen to Mark Fields and complete the missing information in the table.

	Age	Programme(s) he/she likes	Programme(s) he/she doesn't like	Favourite programme	Number of hours a week he/she watches TV
Jane					
Mark				*That 70's Show*	

c 🔊 Listen to the interview with Mark again. <u>Underline</u> the correct words.

1 Mark lives in *Macclesfield / Congleton*.
2 Mark's favourite programme is a *comedy / cartoon*.
3 *That 70's Show* is *a British / an American* TV programme.
4 He usually watches *3 or 4 / 5 or 6* hours of TV each week.
5 Mark usually watches more TV *at the weekend / on weekdays*.

d Do you think that 16-year-olds in your country are similar to Jane and Mark, or different? Why?

11 Write

a There's a TV survey in your school magazine. Read Pavel's paragraph about what programmes he watches and how often.

> I watch TV every weekend and sometimes after school. I like game shows, and my favourite programme is *The Jackpot*. I like it because it's interesting and funny. I usually watch it once a week. I never watch soaps because I think they're boring, and I don't like cartoons at all because my brother always watches them!

b Write about you. Use Pavel's paragraph and your notes from this unit to help you.

Module 2 **Check your progress**

1 **Grammar**

a Complete the sentences about London. Use *There are / Are there / There's / Is there*.

1 *There are* over 300 museums in London.

2 .... a great market in Camden.

3 .... river boat tours every day.

4 .... a post office in Oxford Street?

5 .... any parks in London?

6 .... any good shops in your town? [5]

b Complete the sentences with words from the box.

| (has) 's got (+) | (have) 've got (+) |
| hasn't got (−) | haven't got (−) |

1 My mother *'s got* fair hair. (+)

2 Jim and Ashley are brothers, but they .... the same colour eyes. (−)

3 Sandra and Kate .... two brothers and a sister. (+)

4 I .... a new bicycle, but I hate it. (+)

5 I .... a brother or a sister. (−)

6 He .... a computer at home. (−) [5]

c Complete the sentences with words from the box.

this   that   these   those

1 I'd like ___this___ apple.   3 I'd like .... carrots.

2 I'd like .... bananas.   4 I'd like .... sandwich.

[3]

d Read the dialogue. Write a word from the box in the spaces.

a   an   some

A: Hello, what would you like?
B: Hi. I'd like ___a___ kilo of rice and [1]................ sugar, please.
A: Anything else?
B: Yes, and [2]................ eggs, please.
A: OK, that's six Euros, please.
B: Oh, and I'd like [3]................ apple, and [4]................ banana, please.

[4]

e Complete the sentences with the correct form of the verbs in the box.

go   ~~watch~~   play   eat

1 My Mum *watches* the TV news at nine.
2 Tom usually .... swimming at the weekend.
3 Paul sometimes .... football with his cousin.
4 We always .... fish on Fridays. [3]

(f) Match the two parts of the sentence.

1 Listen   a this book.
2 Read   b down please.
3 Sit   c money here.
4 Come   d to me.
5 Change   e with us.   [ ] 4

2 Vocabulary

(a) Write the numbers.

1 67   _sixty-seven_
2 1000   ....
3 84   ....
4 13   ....
5 19   ....
6 100   ....
7 90   ....   [ ] 6

(b) Write the words from the box in three lists.

arm	yellow	butter	chicken	red
finger	sugar	~~green~~	mouth	black
hand	~~tomatoes~~	head	blue	
orange	beef	eggs	~~foot~~	

Parts of the body	Colours	Food
....	....	....
....	....	....
....	....	....
....	....	....
....	....	....
....	....	....

[ ] 15

(c) Write the days of the week.

1 T h u r s d a y
2 S _ _ _ _ _
3 M _ _ _ _ _
4 W _ _ _ _ _ _ _
5 T _ _ _ _ _ _
6 S _ _ _ _ _ _ _
7 F _ _ _ _ _   [ ] 16

3 Everyday English

Complete the dialogues with the expressions in the box.

| You're welcome   What's wrong |
| Wait a minute   ~~I'm really hungry~~ |
| Are you sure   Do you think so |
| I have no idea |

1 Sue: I've got nothing to eat and
   1 _I'm really hungry_ !

   Ben: Would you like my apple?

   Sue: 2 ....? You've only got
   one.

   Ben: Yes. Here you are.

   Sue: Great, thanks.

   Ben: 3 ....

2 Maria: When does the English lesson
   begin?

   Elise: 4 .... Ten o'clock?
   Eleven o'clock?

   Maria: I've got it in my notebook .
   5 .... Oh no, it's at nine
   o'clock and we're late!

3 Helen: Are you OK?

   Jill: No, I'm not.

   Helen: 6 .... ?

   Jill: My teacher hates me.

   Helen: 7 .... ? I'm sure he
   doesn't.   [ ] 6

How did you do?

Tick (✓) a box for each section.

Total score [ ] 57	☺ Very good	☺ OK	☹ Not very good
Grammar	19 – 24	14 – 18	less than 14
Vocabulary	22 – 27	17 – 21	less than 17
Everyday English	4 – 6	3	less than 3

Module 3
Free time

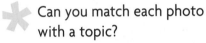

YOU WILL LEARN ABOUT ...

- An athlete in a wheelchair   ....3....
- Sports in British schools   ....
- American festivals   ....
- A London carnival   ....

  ✳ Can you match each photo with a topic?

YOU WILL LEARN HOW TO ...

Speak
- Describe your feelings
- Interview a partner about things they can do
- Talk about your house or flat
- Interview your partner about clothes

Write
- A letter or email about people in your school
- An email about sports you like doing
- A postcard to a friend
- An email about a festival in your country

Read
- A letter to a boyfriend
- An article about an athlete in a wheelchair
- An article about sports in British schools
- A dialogue about present activities
- An article about American festivals
- An article about the Notting Hill carnival

Listen
- A story
- A song
- Information about abilities
- A dialogue about sports
- Sounds of people doing things
- Descriptions of clothing
- A dialogue in a shop

Use grammar

Can you match the names of the grammar points with the examples?

Negative imperatives   I **like watching** tennis on TV.

can/can't for ability   The film starts **at** 8.30.

like/don't like + -ing   Kangaroos **can hop** 10 metres.

Present continuous   **Can** I try them on?

Prepositions   **Don't walk** on the grass!

can/can't for permission   I'm **having** my lunch.

Use vocabulary

Can you think of two more examples for each topic?

Feelings	Sports	House/furniture	Months	Clothes
angry	play tennis	kitchen	October	T-shirt
bored	ski	table	December	shoes
....	....	....	....	....
....	....	....	....	....

 # Don't close the door!

* Negative imperatives
* Vocabulary: adjectives to describe feelings

1 Listen

a 🔊 Look at the pictures. Who are the people in picture a, do you think? Why is the girl angry in picture c? Listen and check your ideas.

b 🔊 Put the pictures in the correct order. Write 2–6 in the boxes. Then listen again and check.

2 Grammar

Negative imperatives

a 🔊 Look at these sentences from the story on page 64. Who says them, Anna or Martin? Write A or M in the boxes. Then listen to the story again and check your answers.

1 Hang on a minute.
2 Don't close the door.
3 Go away!
4 Don't shout.

b Complete the rule.

> **Rule:** Negative imperatives use .... + verb (base form without *to*).

c Look at the drawings. What are the people saying?
Use the verbs from the box.

go away   laugh   cry   ~~shout~~

1 Don't *shout*   2 _____

3 _____   4 _____

d Match the two parts to make sentences 1–5, then match with signs a–e. Write 1–5 in the boxes.

1 Don't park   this door!
2 Don't use   the water!
3 Don't walk   your car here!
4 Don't open   on the grass!
5 Don't drink   your mobile phone!

3 Pronunciation
Linking sounds

a 🔊 Listen to the four sentences from this unit. Can you hear the *t* in *don't*?

Don't laugh.
Don't cry.
Don't shout.
I don't like hamburgers.

b 🔊 Listen to these sentences. Can you hear the *t* in *don't*? Listen again and repeat.

Don't open the door.
Don't eat that.
I don't understand.

1 _____confused_____   2 _____

3 _____   4 _____

5 _____   6 _____

7 _____   8 _____

4 Vocabulary
How do you feel?

a 🔊 Match pictures 1–8 with the words in the box. Write the words in the spaces. Then listen, check and repeat.

> bored   happy   excited
> angry   worried   scared
> sad   confused

b 🔊 Listen to these six people. How do they feel?

1 _____angry_____
2 _____
3 _____
4 _____
5 _____
6 _____

5 Speak

Work with a partner. How do you feel?

1 You have a test tomorrow morning.
   A: *How do you feel?*
   B: *I'm worried!*

2 It's the first day of the summer holidays.

3 You can't do your English homework.

4 You hear strange noises late at night.

5 Your team is in the final match!

6 Your friend says something bad about you.

6 Read

a Read Anna's letter to Martin.

Dear Martin

I'm confused and I'm still angry. First you tell me that you love me, then you tell me you don't. In your letter, you say you still want me to be your girlfriend. Well, I'm sorry, but it's too late. I don't love you now. Don't visit me again. Don't write and don't call.

I've got a new boyfriend, so leave me alone. It's all over for us.

Goodbye

Anna

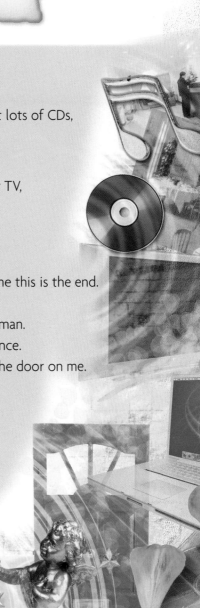

b Mark the sentences *T* (true) or *F* (false).

1 Anna's not angry now. ☐
2 Martin doesn't love Anna. ☐
3 Anna wants Martin to contact her. ☐
4 Anna's got a new boyfriend. ☐

7 Listen

A song

a 🔊 Listen to the song. Write words from the box in the spaces.

> Don't close (x3)
> Don't tell (x2)
> Don't shout   Don't break

b Tell your partner what you think about the song.

¹_____ *the door on me*

I've got a new computer, I've got lots of CDs,
I've got everything that I need
but I haven't got you.

I've got a fancy car, and a colour TV,
I've got everything that I need
but I haven't got you.

Refrain:
²_____ my heart, ³_____ me this is the end.
⁴_____ at me,
⁵_____ me you've got a new man.
Oh, baby give me one more chance.
⁶_____ the door, ⁷_____ the door on me.

I eat in the best restaurants.
And I sleep in top hotels.
Everyone tells me I'm great.
I've got everything that I want,
but I haven't got you.

I miss San Francisco

8 Read and listen

a Where is Amy? Who is the woman? Read, listen and check your answers.

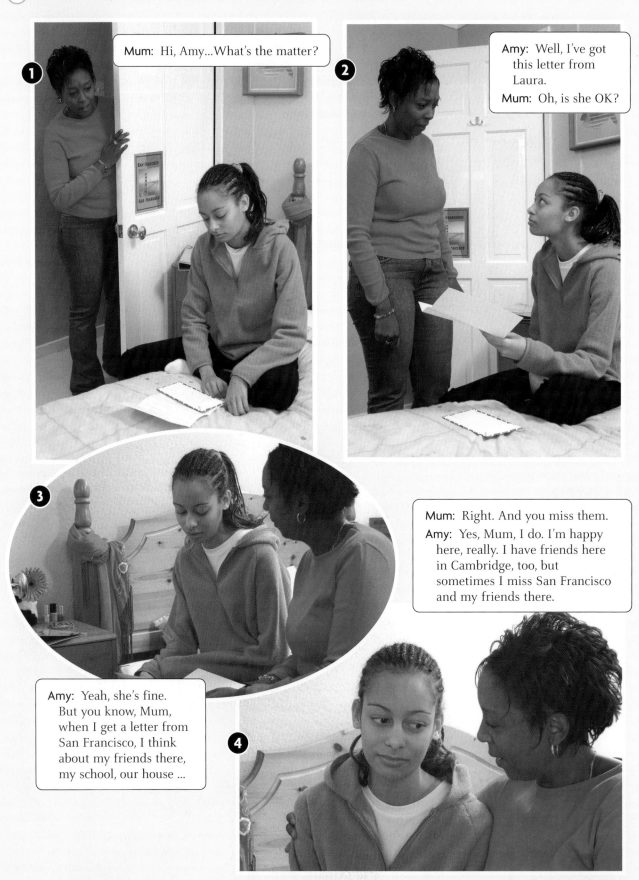

1

Mum: Hi, Amy...What's the matter?

2

Amy: Well, I've got this letter from Laura.
Mum: Oh, is she OK?

3

Amy: Yeah, she's fine. But you know, Mum, when I get a letter from San Francisco, I think about my friends there, my school, our house ...

Mum: Right. And you miss them.
Amy: Yes, Mum, I do. I'm happy here, really. I have friends here in Cambridge, too, but sometimes I miss San Francisco and my friends there.

4

b Read the story again and listen. Circle the correct answers, a or b.

1 Is Amy OK?
  a No.
  b Yes and no.

2 Where does Amy live now?
  a Cambridge.
  b San Francisco.

3 Where does Laura live?
  a Cambridge.
  b San Francisco.

4 How does Amy feel about Cambridge?
  a She is happy, but she misses San Francisco.
  b She is unhappy because she hasn't got friends in Cambridge.

9 Everyday English

a Find these expressions in the story. Who says them? How do you say them in your language?

1 What's the matter?
2 She's fine.
3 I miss San Francisco.

b Read the dialogues. Fill in the spaces with expressions from Exercise 9a.

1 Jane: I always _____ my boyfriend when I go on holiday.
  Alicia: But you speak to him on the phone every day!

2 Markus: Hi Tom! How's your brother now?
  Tom: He _____ thanks.

3 Julie: _____ , Sara? You look really sad!
  Sara: Oh, I'm OK, thanks.

10 Write

a You get an email from an old friend. Who is new in her school? What questions does she ask?

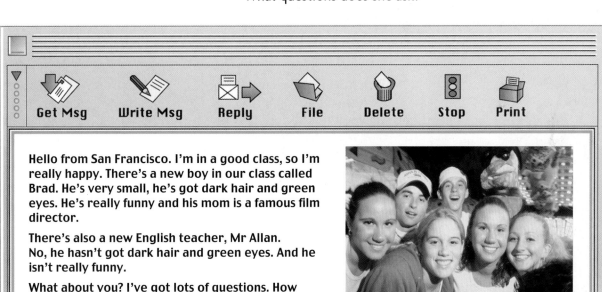

Get Msg Write Msg Reply File Delete Stop Print

Hello from San Francisco. I'm in a good class, so I'm really happy. There's a new boy in our class called Brad. He's very small, he's got dark hair and green eyes. He's really funny and his mom is a famous film director.

There's also a new English teacher, Mr Allan. No, he hasn't got dark hair and green eyes. And he isn't really funny.

What about you? I've got lots of questions. How are you? How are things at your school? Are your friends fun? Are your teachers interesting? Are you happy there?

Mail me soon!

PS Here's a photo of me with my friends. Don't forget me!

b Write to your old friend about these things:
  ● your friends (hair, eyes, etc. / funny, wonderful, nice)
  ● one thing you like about your school or teachers
  ● one thing you don't like

10 We can't lose

* *can/can't* (ability)
* *like / don't like -ing*
* Vocabulary: sports

1 Read and listen

a Look at the pictures. Who do you think the man in the wheelchair is? Who is the man pushing him? Read the article and check your answers.

'WE NEVER WIN BUT WE ALWAYS WIN'

Rick Hoyt is American. He has a good job at the University of Boston. Rick is in a wheelchair because he's got cerebral palsy. Rick can't talk, so he uses a computer to talk to people. He also loves sport, and he takes part in triathlons.

In the triathlon, people swim four kilometres, cycle 180 kilometres and run 42 kilometres. Rick can't run, cycle or swim because he's in a wheelchair. So how can he take part in a triathlon?

Rick can take part because he does it with his father, Dick Hoyt. In the running, his father pushes him in his wheelchair. In the swimming, Rick lies in a small boat and his father swims and pulls him. And in the cycling, Rick sits in a special seat on the front of his father's bike.

Of course, the Hoyts never win the race. The winner of a triathlon usually finishes in about nine hours. The Hoyts always take about 15 or 16 hours. 'That's right,' says Dick. 'We never win. But Rick and I think that we always win.'

b 🔊 Read the article again and listen. Answer the questions.

1 How does Rick talk to people?
2 What do people do in a triathlon?
3 How does Rick's father help him in a triathlon?
4 How long do Rick and Dick take to finish a triathlon?
5 Why do you think Dick says, 'Rick and I think that we always win.'

2 Grammar

can/can't (ability)

a Look at the examples. How do you say these sentences in your language?

*Rick **can't** talk.*
*How **can** Rick take part in a triathlon?*

b Look at the text on page 70 again. <u>Underline</u> other examples with *can* or *can't*.

c Complete the table.

Positive	Negative	Question	Short answer
I/you/we/they/he/she/it **can** swim.	I/you/we/they/he/she/it .... (**cannot**) swim.	.... I/you/we/they/he/she/it swim?	Yes, I/you/we/they/he/she/it **can**.
			No, I/you/we/they/he/she/it .... (**cannot**).

d Make sentences.

1 John + understand Russian / – speak it
   He can understand Russian but he can't speak it .

2 Claire + ride a bike / – swim
   She .

3 Chimpanzees + learn to count / – learn to speak English
   They .

4 I + use a computer / – draw pictures with it
   I .

5 She + play the guitar / – play the violin
   She .

3 Listen

Listen and mark the statements *T* (true) or *F* (false).

1 Camels can live without water for 16 months. ☐
2 People can see one million different colours. ☐
3 Kangaroos can hop 100 metres. ☐
4 A man from the USA can eat 94 worms in 30 seconds. ☐
5 A man from Cuba can go down to 162 metres under water
   without oxygen. ☐

4 Pronunciation

can/can't

a Listen to the sentences. What's the difference between the sounds in *can* /ə/ and *can't* /ɑː/?

1 He can write on a computer, but he can't walk.

2 She can ride a bike, but she can't swim.

3 They can learn to count, but they can't learn to talk.

4 I can use a computer, but I can't draw pictures with it.

b Listen again and repeat.

c Listen to the short conversations. Then listen again and repeat.

1 A: *Can you swim?*
   B: *No, I can't.*

2 A: *Can you sing?*
   B: *Yes, but not very well!*

5 Speak

Work with a partner. Ask and answer questions using the words in the box. Add two more questions.

A: *Can you swim?*

B: *Yes, I can, but not very well. Can you play the piano?*

A: *No, I can't.*

swim	play the piano	juggle	walk on your hands
use a computer	sing	.... ?	

Look

A: *Can you swim?*

B: *Yes, **but not very well.**
= Yes, but I'm not very good.*

6 Vocabulary

Sports

 Match the words from the box with the pictures. Write the words in the spaces. Then listen, check and repeat.

play tennis
do gymnastics
snowboard
ride a horse
play volleyball
play football
ski
play basketball
rollerblade

1 *play volleyball*   2 ....   3 ....

4 ....   5 ....   6 ....

7 ....   8 ....   9 ....

7 Listen

a 🔊 Listen to the conversation between Amy and Alex. Tick (✓) the sports they talk about.

volleyball

American football

swimming

tennis

basketball

football (soccer)

rollerblading

gymnastics

b 🔊 Listen again. Mark the statements *T* (true) or *F* (false).

1 Amy goes roller-blading every day. ☐

2 Alex likes playing tennis, but he doesn't like watching it on TV. ☐

3 Amy likes watching American football games. ☐

4 Alex plays football in his school team. ☐

8 Grammar

like / don't like -ing

a Look at the examples and the table. Then complete the rule.

I **like watching** tennis on TV.
I **don't like playing** it.
I **love going** to the games.

Positive	Negative	Question	Short answer
I really like swimming. I love watching tennis on TV. I hate playing football.	I don't like cycling.	Do you like playing games?	Yes, I do. No, I don't.

Rule: When you talk about activities, use the *-ing* form of the verb, after the verbs .... , ... and ....

b Work with a partner. Ask and answer questions. Use the verbs in the box.

A: *Do you like watching football on TV?*
B: *Yes, I watch it twice a week.*

> play volleyball   watch football on TV   do homework
> get up early   swim   go to the cinema   dance

c Put the words in the correct order.

1 like tennis We playing don't
We don't like playing tennis .

2 going the like to cinema She doesn't
....

3 like your Do on going parents holiday?
....

4 really soccer brother likes watching His
....

5 swimming hate in I sea the
....

Culture in mind

9 Read

a) Match the names of the sports with the photos. Write 1–6 in boxes a–f.

1 netball
2 hockey
3 swimming
4 football
5 rugby
6 cricket

b) Read about Miriam and Jack and write their names under the photos of the sports they play.

c) Read the web page again and complete the sentences. Write *Miriam* or *Jack* in the spaces.

1 .... does four hours of sports every week.

2 .... has three hours of PE every week.

3 .... doesn't play football for the school team.

4 .... plays football and rugby in winter.

5 .... goes to Europe every summer.

6 .... goes swimming twice a week.

d) Look at the fact box. How many British teenagers do sports regularly? Which sports are popular with teenagers in Britain?

Sport in British school

We spoke to two typical British teenagers to find out about the sports they do at school.

Miriam Jackson is a Year 11 (ages 15–16) student at Bournemouth High School in the south of England. She has three hours of PE (Physical Education) at school every week. In the winter she usually plays netball and hockey. In the summer she plays tennis.

Outside school, Miriam plays football every Saturday for a local girls' team. She also goes swimming twice a week.

Jack Shone is a Year 10 student at the Sacred Heart School in Droitwich in the Midlands. He has four hours of sports at school every week. He plays football and rugby in the winter, and cricket and tennis in the summer. Jack is a member of his school's football and cricket teams. They usually play matches on Saturday mornings. Every summer the football team goes to Europe to play against teams from other countries.

c

d

e

f

FACT BOX

Do typical British teenagers do a lot of sports? What kinds of sports do they do? We did a survey to find out. It seems that British teenagers don't spend all their free time watching TV! Here are some facts.

- **70% of British school children do sport regularly.**
- **The average British teenager does 8.1 hours of sport every week.**
- **51% of British school children swim regularly.**
- **49% of British school children cycle regularly.**
- **37% of British school children play football regularly.**

10 Write

(a) Read this email from Javed, an English boy. What's his favourite football team?

> **Dear ....**
>
> **Thank you for your email! I really like reading about your family and friends.**
>
> **At school we've got a new sports hall. That's great for us because it's often cold or wet here! In England we love football. At school we usually play football but sometimes we play tennis. I don't really like tennis, because I can't play it! But I love playing football (I think I'm quite good at it!). I like watching it on TV too. I support Liverpool, they're fantastic!**
>
> **Do you like sports? Please write and tell me about the sports you do in your country and the sports you like and don't like.**
>
> **Please write soon!**
>
> **Javed**

(b) Answer Javed's email. Write about:

- popular sports in your country
- sports you do at school
- sports you like / sports you don't like
- your favourite football team or your favourite sports star

11 Reading on the roof!

✳ Present continuous
✳ Vocabulary: house and furniture

1 Read and listen

a Look at the pictures and answer the questions. Then read the conversation and check your ideas.

1 Where is Kate? Why is she happy?
2 Where is Ben? Why is he unhappy?

Kate: Oh, hello Ben!

Ben: Hi Kate! How's your holiday?

Kate: Great thanks.

Ben: What are you doing today?

Kate: Well, at the moment I'm reading on the roof! It's really sunny and we're having a great time. Dad's playing cards with Jess in the dining room.

Ben: You've got a dining room?

Kate: Well, there's a table in the kitchen, two bedrooms, a shower and a toilet! Mum loves it. She's taking pictures.

Ben: Hmm. I'm looking after Jamie.

Kate: Is the weather nice there too?

Ben: It's OK. I'm sitting in the garden, but I'm not having a great time. I hate babysitting.

Kate: Oh well, sorry I can't help!

Ben: Yeah well ... have a good time! See you.

Kate: Bye!

b 🔊 Read the text again and listen. Match the people with the activities.

1 Kate	a is baby sitting.
2 Kate's dad	b is taking pictures.
3 Kate's mum	c is reading.
4 Ben	d is playing in the garden.
5 Jamie	e is playing cards.

2 Grammar

Present continuous

a Look at the examples. <u>Underline</u> other examples of the present continuous in the conversation on page 76. Then complete the rule and the table.

I'm reading on the roof!
We're having a great time.

Look

Spelling
have – having
make – making
shop – shopping

Positive	Negative	Question	Short answer
I'm (am) reading.	I'm not read........ .	........I read........ ?	Yes, I .... / No, I ....
You/we/they........ (are) reading.	You/we/they .... (are not) read........ .	.... you/we/they read........ ?	Yes, you/we/they .... No, you/we/they ....
He/she/(it)........ (is) reading.	He/she/(it) .... (is not) read........ .	.... he/she/(it) read........... ?	Yes, he/she .... No, he/she ....

Rule: We use the .... to talk about things that are happening now.

b Complete the sentences with the present continuous form of the verbs.

1 A: Can I talk to Caroline?
   B: No, sorry. She's in her bedroom.
      She *'s writing*........... a letter. (write)

2 A: Mum, where's Dad?
   B: He's in the bathroom.
      He .... a shower. (have)

3 A: Where's John?
   B: He's in the park. He ....
      football with his friends. (play)

4 A: Can you help me?
   B: Not right now. I .... my lunch. (have)

5 A: Where are you?
   B: I'm in a bookshop in town. I
      .... my sister a book. (buy)

c Make questions and answers with the present continuous.

1 he / go to school?/ no / come home
   Is he going to school? No, he isn't.
   He's coming home.

2 they / eat ice creams? / no / drink milkshakes
   ....
   ....

3 she / read a book? / no / listen to a CD
   ....
   ....

4 your father / work today? / no / have a day off
   ....
   ....

3 Listen

🔊 Listen to six sounds. What are the people doing?

1 She _'s cleaning her teeth_ .
2 He _____ .
3 They _____ .
4 She _____ .
5 He _____ .
6 They _____ .

4 Speak and write

(a) Look at the pictures, and write sentences about the people. Then work with a partner and read your sentences aloud.

Rob's playing football.

(b) Work with a partner. Cover your sentences and ask and answer questions about the people in the pictures.

A: *Is Lucy playing football?*
B: *No, she isn't, she's reading. Are Rob and Amy ... ?*

(c) Work with a partner. Say where your friends and family are now, and what they are doing.

A: *My brother's at work. I think he's talking on the phone.*
B: *My mum and dad are going to work and my sister's at school. I think she's studying Maths now.*

5 Pronunciation

/h/ *have*

🔊 Listen and repeat the sentences.

1 Hi! Can I help you?
2 He can walk on his hands.
3 Are you hungry? Have a hamburger.
4 Henry's having a holiday in Holland.

Vocabulary
House and furniture

◁») Match the words in the boxes with the numbers and letters in the picture.
Write the letters and numbers next to the words. Then listen, check and repeat.

kitchen ..1.. garden .... hall .... living room .... bathroom .... bedroom ....

door .... sofa .... armchair .... cooker .... chairs .... fridge ....
window ..a.. table .... bed .... bath .... shower .... toilet ....

Look

Prepositions

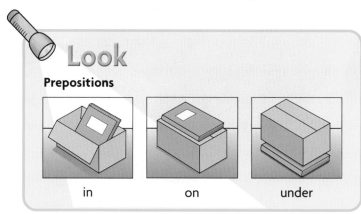

in   on   under

7 Speak

Work with a partner. Talk about your house or flat.

There's a fridge and a cooker in the kitchen. The TV's on a table in the living room. We haven't got a garden.

I'm on my way!

8 Read and listen

a Where is Lucy in picture 1? Where is she in picture 4? Read, listen and check your answers.

Sunday afternoon.

1

Alex: Hi, Lucy. What are you doing?
Lucy: Nothing much. I'm just writing some emails.
Alex: Well, come round to my place. We're watching DVDs.
Lucy: I'm on my way!

2

Rob: Lucy, hi! Where are you going?
Lucy: I'm going to Alex's place. They're watching DVDs. What are you up to?
Rob: I'm going to my cousins' house. They're having a party.
Lucy: OK. See you.

3

Alex: Lucy! Hi!
Lucy: But Alex – what about the DVDs?
Amy: Oh, we're playing Air Football now.

4

Lucy: Oh, great. Air Football. My favourite!

b Answer the questions.

1 What's Lucy doing in picture 1?
2 What are Alex and Amy doing in picture 3?
3 Why is Lucy unhappy in picture 4?

9 Everyday English

a Find these expressions in the photo story. Who says them? How do you say them in your language?

1 Come round to my place.
2 I'm on my way.
3 What are you up to?
4 See you.

b Write an expression from Exercise 9a in the spaces.

1 **Aline:** I don't know what to do. Any ideas?
Ben: Yeah. I've got some new computer games at home. .... and we can play them.
Aline: OK, ...!

2 **Susie:** Hi Harry! ....?
Harry: I'm going to see a film. Do you want to come?
Susie: Sorry, I can't. I'm going to my grandmother's house for lunch.
Harry: OK, ...

10 Write

a Claire is on holiday in Portugal with her family. Read her postcard to Alex, and then answer the questions.

Dear Alex,

Here I am in Portugal! I'm having a great time here. The weather's fantastic – really sunny and warm. We're staying in a small hotel near the beach. The hotel's got a swimming pool – great! My parents aren't here right now – they're doing some shopping in the town. So I'm here alone, and I'm having breakfast – in the sun!

Hope you're OK – see you soon.

Love

Claire

Alex Campbell
336 Hills Road
CAMBRIDGE
CB1 4XY
United Kingdom

1 Where is the hotel?
2 Why does Claire like the hotel?
3 Where are Claire's parents?
4 What is Claire doing?
5 What's the weather like?

Look

What's the weather like?

It's raining.   It's cloudy.   It's sunny.

b You are having a holiday with your family. Write a postcard to your English-speaking penfriend. Use Claire's postcard and the questions to help you.

Where's the hotel?
What are you doing?
What's the weather like?

12 Can I try them on?

* *can/can't* (asking for permission)
* Prepositions: *at, in, on*
* *one/ones*
* Vocabulary: months of the year and seasons, clothes

1 Read and listen

(a) Look at the pictures. Do you know the names of any American festivals? Match the pictures with the festivals. Write 1–3 in the boxes next to the pictures a–c. Then read the article and check your answers.

CANADA

UNITED STATES OF AMERICA

Chicago
Baltimore New York

New Orleans

Americans love to party!

Come and visit the USA!

Do you want to see festivals, parades and parties? There are lots of them in the States. There is something special almost every month of the year. Here are some of the things you can see.

1 **St Patrick's Day** Every year on 17 March, many people in big cities like New York, Chicago and Baltimore go onto the streets in a big parade for St Patrick's Day. This is an important holiday for the millions of Irish Americans. The national colour of Ireland is green, so many people wear green clothes: hats, scarves, sweaters, skirts, trousers and so on.

2 **Mardi Gras** The wonderful city of New Orleans is famous all over the world for two things: jazz and Mardi Gras. Mardi Gras is a two-week carnival in February or March. There is music in the streets, people wear colourful clothes and they sing and dance all day and all night.

3 **Thanksgiving** Thanksgiving Day is an important holiday in America. Every year, on the last Thursday in November, people have parades everywhere in the USA. There is a big parade in the streets of New York. It is a very colourful parade with music and big balloons of famous cartoon characters. In the evening, people have Thanksgiving dinner. They eat turkey and pumpkin pie.

(b) 🔊 Read the article again and listen. Write the names of the festivals.

1 People wear special clothes. ....
2 People eat turkey. ....
3 There is music and dancing at night. ....

2 Vocabulary

Months of the year and seasons

a 🔊 Listen and underline the syllables with the main stress. Then listen, check and repeat.

January

February

March

April

May

June

July

August

September

October

November

December

b Find examples of the months in the article on page 82 and underline them.

c 🔊 Match the names of the seasons with the pictures. Write a–d in the boxes. Then listen, check and repeat.

a summer b winter c spring d autumn

d Which season goes with which months? What's your favourite season? Why?

3 Grammar and speaking

Prepositions

a Study the examples in the table.

at	in	on
7 o'clock 9.30	June March summer winter	Monday Tuesday

b Write words from the box in the spaces.

on   in   at

1 The film starts .... 8.30 tonight.
2 I have English lessons .... Monday, Wednesday and Friday.
3 My mother's birthday is .... June.
4 We usually go to my grandparents' house .... spring.

c Work with a partner. Tell each other true things about you. Use the prepositions from the box in Exercise 3b.

My birthday is in June.
My best friend's birthday is in April.
I usually get up at 5.30, but on Sunday I get up at 10.
I always go to the cinema on Saturday.

4 Vocabulary

Clothes

a 🔊 Match the names of the clothes with the picture. Write 1–12 in the boxes. Then listen, check and repeat.

1 T shirt	2 scarf	3 shirt	4 dress	5 trousers	6 jumper
7 socks	8 jacket	9 top	10 jeans	11 shoes	12 trainers

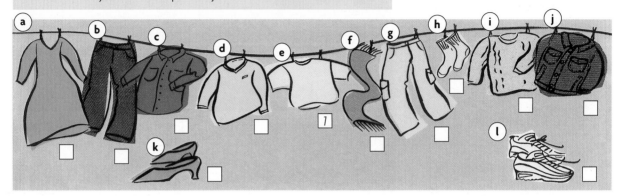

b Read the article in Exercise 1 on page 82 again. <u>Underline</u> all the words for clothes.

5 Listen

🔊 Listen and number the pictures 1–4.

6 Speak

a Work with a partner. Find a picture in one of the stories in this book. Say what the person is wearing, but don't say the person's name! Can your partner find the same picture?

A: *She's wearing a white T-shirt, black trousers and white trainers.*

B: *It's Amy, on page 24.*

b Work with a partner. Ask and answer the questions. Write down your partner's answers.

- How often do you go shopping for clothes?
- What kinds of clothes do you like?
- Do you like shopping for clothes? Why / Why not?
- What are your favourite shops?
- Do you like shopping alone, or with your friends?

7 Pronunciation

/æ/ and /e/

a 🔊 Listen and repeat the words.

/æ/	/e/
black	yes
jacket	red
hamburger	dress
thanks	yellow
January	September

b 🔊 Say the sentences. Then listen and repeat.

1 I like the black jacket in the window.
2 I wear red in January and yellow in September.
3 She's wearing a black and red dress.

Grammar

can/can't (asking for permission)

a Read the two conversations. What do the people want to buy?

1 Man: Hi. You've got some black trainers in the window. Can I try them on?

   Assistant: The black ones? Yes, of course you can. What size?

   Man: 42.

   Assistant: OK. Just a moment.

2 Assistant: Hi! Can I help you?

   Woman: Yes. Can I have that green shirt please?

   Assistant: What size?

   Woman: Er, large I think.

   Assistant: Sorry, we haven't got any of the green ones in large.

b Look at the example. When do we use *can I ...*?

Can I try them on?

c Underline other examples of *can I ...* in the dialogues in Exercise 8a.

d Listen to the dialogues and number the pictures 1–4.

(a)

(b)

(c)

(d)

e Listen to two of the dialogues again and write the missing words in the spaces. Then listen again and repeat.

1 Boy: .... I use your stereo?

   Girl: .... , James. I'm using it.

   Boy: OK.

2 Girl: Is that book good?

   Boy: Yes, it's great.

   Girl: .... I read it?

   Boy: .... ! Here you are!

f Work with a partner. Use the pictures to make conversations.

one/ones

g Look at these examples from the dialogues in Exercise 8a. When do we use *one* and *ones*?

You've got some trainers in the window.
*The black **ones**? (ones = trainers)*

Can I have that green shirt?
*The green **one** is small. (one = shirt)*

h Write *one* or *ones* in the spaces to replace the words which are crossed out.

1 A: *I like those trousers in the window.*

   B: *Which ~~trousers~~   ones   ?*

   A: *The black ~~trousers~~ .... – over there, in the corner.*

2 A: *Can I see the shirt in the window, please?*

   B: *Sorry, which ~~shirt~~ .... ? The green ~~shirt~~ .... ?*

   A: *No, the red ~~shirt~~ ....*

Culture in mind

9 Read

a) Read the text and match the photos on the **page** with the words below. Write 1–5 in the boxes.

1 Typical Jamaican food
2 A carnival costume
3 A steel band
4 A carnival float
5 A sound system

London's carnival

Every year in August there is a huge Caribbean party in London. Nearly two million people come to enjoy the music, dancing and fun of the Notting Hill carnival. Many come from other countries.

The carnival is more than forty years old, and lasts for two days, a Sunday and a Monday. The Sunday is a family day with lots of fun and games for children. On the Monday there is a huge carnival parade called the 'Mas'. This includes about 70 floats and about 3,000 people wearing colourful carnival costumes.

Of course, music is very important. The carnival music is calypso – traditional music from the Caribbean. Steel bands play music from Trinidad and Tobago and a lot of people dance in the street. But calypso isn't the only music. Thirty-five sound systems play dance music around the streets. Every year, the DJs play about 16,000 CDs!

Food is also a big attraction and there are a lot of street stalls selling delicious carnival food.

b Read the text on page 86 again and answer the questions.

1 How many people enjoy the Notting Hill carnival every year?
2 How old is the carnival?
3 How many days does the carnival last?
4 What is the 'Mas'?
5 What kind of music can you hear at the carnival?

c Is there a carnival in your country? What other festivals are there in your country?

10 Write

a Read this email from Steve in the USA. What do young people do at Halloween in the USA?

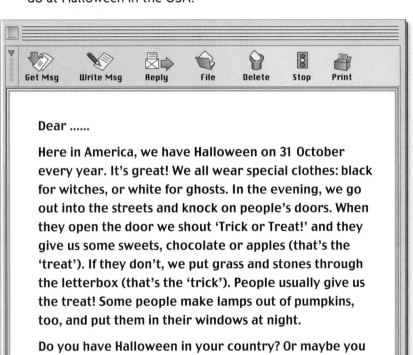

Get Msg   Write Msg   Reply   File   Delete   Stop   Print

Dear ......

Here in America, we have Halloween on 31 October every year. It's great! We all wear special clothes: black for witches, or white for ghosts. In the evening, we go out into the streets and knock on people's doors. When they open the door we shout 'Trick or Treat!' and they give us some sweets, chocolate or apples (that's the 'treat'). If they don't, we put grass and stones through the letterbox (that's the 'trick'). People usually give us the treat! Some people make lamps out of pumpkins, too, and put them in their windows at night.

Do you have Halloween in your country? Or maybe you have other festivals, with special clothes and food? Can you write and tell me about it? I'd love to know what you do there!

Write soon!

Steve

b Write an email to Steve. Write about a special festival in your country. Use the questions to make notes first.

● What's the festival called?
● When is it?
● What do people do? (music, clothes, food, parades)

Use your notes and Steve's email to help you.

Module 3 Check your progress

1 Grammar

a Write the words in the correct order.

1 don't / playing / like / I / tennis
I don't like playing tennis.

2 on / soaps / watching / you / Do / TV / like

3 My / swimming / sea / in / brother / likes / the

4 cat / Her / milk / doesn't / drinking / like

☐ 3

b Write sentences about what the people *can* and *can't* do.

1 I _____*can juggle*_____ (+ juggle) but _____*I can't swim*_____ (– swim).

2 My dad _____ (+ stand on his head) and _____ (+ walk on his hands).

3 Tessa _____ (+ play football) but _____ (– rollerblade).

4 Kylie and Annie _____ (– sing) but _____ (+ dance).

☐ 3

c Complete the sentences. Use the verbs from the box with *Can*.

| borrow | ~~close~~ | open | play | try on |

1 I'm cold! _____*Can*_____ I _____*close*_____ the door, please?

2 _____ my son _____ this shirt, please?

3 It's so hot in here. _____ we _____ the window, please?

4 _____ they _____ their new CD now? It's really good!

5 Jack, you've got two pencils. _____ I _____ one, please?

☐ 4

d Complete the dialogues. Use the present continuous.

1 A: Hi, Liz. What ____*are*____ you ____*doing*____ ? (do)
   B: I _____ (read a book)

2 A: Can I talk to Claudia, please?
   B: No, sorry. She _____ (have a shower)

3 A: Are Peter and Angela here?
   B: Yes. They're in the living room. They _____ (watch TV)

4 A: Where's Rick?
   B: He's in Emma's room. He _____ (look for a CD)

☐ 4

e Complete the sentences with *one* or *ones*.

1 A: I'd like that scarf, please.
   B: This _____*one*_____ ?
   A: No, the blue _____ .

2 I don't like my jeans, I'd like some new _____ .

3 I want some socks. How much are the blue and white _____ ?

☐ 3

f Complete the sentences. Use *in*, *on* or *at*.

1 The shop opens _____ nine o'clock.

2 We never go to school _____ Saturday.

3 My grandmother is coming to see us _____ the weekend.

4 They like going skiing _____ winter.

☐ 4

g Underline the correct words.

1 The phone's ringing! *Don't answer / Answer* it for me, please!

2 Great to see you! *Don't come / Come* again!

3 *Don't watch / Watch* the football tonight! I want to see a film.

4 *Don't write / Write* to her soon! She misses you.

☐ 3

2 Vocabulary

a Write the words in the lists.

> June   summer   ~~spring~~   August   ~~December~~
> winter   autumn   April

Months	Seasons
December	*spring*
....	....
....	....
....	....

☐ 6

b Put the letters in order to find six more clothes.

1 hitrs   *shirt*
2 rssruote   ....
3 fsrac   ....
4 sserd   ....
5 rempuj   ....
6 ocssk   ....
7 airestrn   ....
8 aht   ....
9 ajkect   ....

☐ 8

c Write the names of rooms and furniture in a house.

1 ___*kitchen*___
2 f ___ d ___ e
3 ___ i ___ i ___ g ___ o ___ m
4 t ___ le
5 ba ___ ___ r ___ ___ ___
6 ___ h ___ w ___ ___
7 ___ ___ f ___
8 ___ e ___ ___ ___ m
9 ___ ___ o ___ e ___

☐ 8

d Underline the correct word.

1 I'm *excited/confused*. I don't understand this homework.
2 Don't shout at me! Why are you so *angry/bored*?
3 She's really *worried/excited* – it's her birthday today!
4 He's *scared/bored* because it's a really long lesson.
5 She's crying. Why is she so *happy/unhappy*?

☐ 4

3 Everyday English

Complete the dialogues with the expressions in the box.

> ~~What's the matter~~   What are you up to
> I miss her   See you
> Come round to my place   I'm on my way

Ben: Oh, hi Sam. It's Ben. How are you?
Sam: Awful.
Ben: Why? [1] *What's the matter* ?
Sam: My girlfriend's on holiday and [2] _____ .
Ben: Well, [3] _____ at the moment?
Sam: Nothing. I'm just sitting here.
Ben: Listen. I've got some new DVDs. [4] _____ and we can watch them together.
Sam: Great idea! [5] _____ .
Ben: OK. [6] _____ soon then.

☐ 5

How did you do?

Tick (✓) a box for each section.

Total score	🙂 Very good	😐 OK	☹ Not very good
☐ 55			
Grammar	17 – 24	13 – 16	less than 13
Vocabulary	22 – 26	18 – 21	less than 18
Everyday English	3 – 5	2	less than 2

Module 4
Past and present

YOU WILL LEARN ABOUT ...

- John Lennon 6
- The Beatles ....
- A famous nurse ....
- A South African hero ....
- Lord Lucan ....
- The *Mary Celeste* mystery ....
- A chef from Scotland ....
- Holiday camps in Britain ....

  ✳ **Can you match each photo with a topic?**

YOU WILL LEARN HOW TO ...

Speak
- Interview a partner about family birthdays
- Interview a partner about things they did in the past
- Tell a story
- Make guesses about what things are
- Compare things

Write
- An email about a holiday
- A paragraph about a famous person
- A story about a strange place
- A competition entry

Read
- An article about John Lennon
- A text about Florence Nightingale
- An article about Steve Biko
- An article about Lord Lucan
- A text about the *Mary Celeste*
- An article about a chef
- An article about British holiday camps

Listen
- A dialogue about the Beatles
- A quiz about famous moments in history
- An interview about Lord Lucan
- An interview about life in the 1950s

Use grammar

Can you match the names of the grammar points with the examples?

Past simple *was / wasn't* — She **wanted** to be a nurse.

Past simple *were / weren't* — They **were** in New York.

Past simple regular verbs — No one **knew** where he **went**.

Past simple irregular verbs — Delhi is **hotter** than London.

Comparative adjectives — He **was** only 40.

Use vocabulary

Can you think of two more examples for each topic?

Time expressions	Adverbs	Adjectives
last night	quickly	modern
yesterday	slowly	dangerous
....	....	....
....	....	....

13 He was only 40

* Past simple: *was/wasn't; were/weren't*
* Vocabulary: time expressions; ordinal numbers and dates

1 Read and listen

(a) What do you know about the men in the photos? What are their names and why are they famous? Read the article and check your answers.

(b) 🔊 Read the article again and listen. Mark the statements *T* (true) or *F* (false).

1 Yoko Ono was John Lennon's wife. ☐

2 Mark Chapman was English. ☐

3 There were two shots from the gun. ☐

4 The police were there in five minutes. ☐

There was a man at the door

On 8 December 1980, ex-Beatle John Lennon and his wife Yoko Ono were in New York. In the afternoon, they were on their way to a recording studio to work on a new song. There was an American called Mark Chapman in the street. In his hand, there was a piece of paper and a pen. 'Mr Lennon,' he said. 'Can I have your autograph?' John Lennon signed his name and Chapman went away.

In the evening, John and Yoko were in front of their apartment building. There was a man at the door. It was Mark Chapman. This time, there wasn't a pen in his hand, but a gun. 'Mr Lennon!' he said. Suddenly, there were five shots and John Lennon was dead. He was only 40 years old.

Three minutes later, the police were at the apartment building. Mark Chapman was still there. His only words were: 'I shot John Lennon.'

2 Grammar

Past simple: *was/wasn't; were/weren't*

(a) Look at these examples from the article on page 92 and complete the table.

*John Lennon and his wife Yoko Ono **were** in New York.*

*There **was** a man at the door.*

*This time, there **wasn't** a pen in his hand.*

Positive	Negative	Question	Short answer
I/he/she/it .... late yesterday.	I/he/she/it **wasn't** (.............) late yesterday.	**Was** I/he/she/it late yesterday?	Yes, I/he/she **was**. No, I/he/she ....
We/you/they **were** late yesterday.	We/you/they .... (**were not**) late yesterday.	.... we/you/they late yesterday?	Yes, we/you/they **were**. No, we/you/they **weren't**.

(b) <u>Underline</u> other examples of sentences with the past simple of the verb *be* on page 92.

(c) Complete the sentences with *was* or *were*.

1 ..*Were*.... John Lennon and Yoko Ono in London?
2 .... they on their way to the cinema?
3 .... Mark Chapman in the street?
4 .... John Lennon and Yoko Ono in front of the cinema in the evening?
5 .... Mark Chapman at the door of the apartment?
6 .... there a pen in his hand?
7 .... John Lennon 50 years old?

3 Pronunciation

was/wasn't and *were/weren't*

(a) 🔊 Listen and repeat the sentences.

1 He was only 40.
2 They were in New York.
3 There wasn't a pen in his hand.
4 They weren't in London.

(b) 🔊 Listen and repeat the sentences.

'Was he only 40?' – 'Yes, he was.'

'Were they in London?' – 'No, they weren't.'

(c) Work with a partner. Ask and answer the questions from Exercise 2c.

A: *Were John Lennon and Yoko Ono in London?*

B: *No, they weren't, they were in New York.*

4 Vocabulary and speaking

Time expressions

(a) Write words from the box in the spaces in the table.

evening   afternoon   month   weekend

Last	night	Yesterday	morning
	week		night
	-------------		-------------
	-------------		-------------

(b) Work with a partner. Ask and answer questions about yesterday. Use the times in the box and the time expressions in Exercise 4a. Write your partner's answers.

6 am   9 am   1.30 pm   5 pm
8 pm   11.30 pm

A: *Where were you at six o'clock yesterday morning?*

B: *I was in bed. What about you?*

(c) Tell the class about your partner's day.

Marcia was in bed at 6 am last Saturday morning. At 8 pm she was in the cinema with her friends.

5 Listen

a What do you know about the Beatles? Answer the questions.

1 Where were the Beatles from?
2 How many men were there in the group?
3 What were their names?

b 🔊 Listen and check your answers.

c 🔊 Listen again and mark the statements *T* (true) or *F* (false).

1 John Lennon was Mum's favourite singer. ☐
2 You never hear Beatles songs on the radio now. ☐
3 *Miss You* was a famous Beatles song. ☐
4 The Beatles were still together in 1969. ☐

6 Vocabulary

Ordinal numbers and dates

a Complete the sentence from the text on page 92.

On _____ , ex-Beatle John Lennon and his wife Yoko Ono were in New York.

b 🔊 Listen and repeat.

1st (first)
2nd (second)
3rd (third)
4th (fourth)
5th (fifth)
6th (sixth)
7th (seventh)
8th (eighth)
9th (ninth)
10th (tenth)
12th (twelfth)
13th (thirteenth)
20th (twentieth)
30th (thirtieth)

c 🔊 Listen and write the numbers.

_____3rd_____

_____

_____

_____

_____

_____

_____

_____

d Work with a partner. Ask and answer questions.

A: *What's the first month?*
B: *January. What's the seventh month?*

e 🔊 Listen to four conversations and tick (✓) the dates you hear.

1	a	December 5	b	December 6
2	a	13 June	b	30 June
3	a	4 January	b	14 January
4	a	April 21	b	April 23

f Work with a partner. Ask and answer the questions. Write your partner's answers.

1 When's your birthday?
2 When's your father's birthday?
3 When's your mother's birthday?
4 When's your best friend's birthday?

g How do you say these dates?

27/12/1968 = the twenty-seventh of December nineteen sixty-eight

1 01/03/1999
2 30/11/1978
3 16/01/1985
4 17/10/1974
5 02/02/2003

Look

We write: *(On) 8 December 1980 or 8/12/1980.*

We say: *(On) the eighth of December, nineteen eighty* or
(On) December the eighth nineteen eighty.

Rob's wallet

7 Read and listen

(a) 🔊 What is Rob's problem? Read, listen and check your answer.

1

Rob: Oh, no! My wallet. Where is it?

Amy: OK, Rob. Calm down! Where was your wallet this morning?

Rob: Well, I was in town this morning ... so it was in my jacket pocket.

2

Lucy: Where were you, Rob?

Rob: Well, first I was in the CD shop. Then a bookshop.

Amy: And after that?

Rob: The bank, I think. I'm sure the wallet was in my pocket then.

3

Amy: And then?

Rob: Well, then I was in the sports shop to buy some new trainers. And now here I am!

Lucy: Rob – can I have a look inside the bag?

Rob: The bag?

4

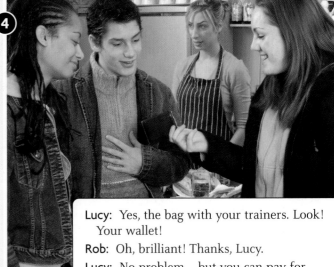

Lucy: Yes, the bag with your trainers. Look! Your wallet!

Rob: Oh, brilliant! Thanks, Lucy.

Lucy: No problem – but you can pay for these now!

Rob: You must be joking!

(b) Look at the sentences. Find one thing that's wrong in every sentence and correct it.

1 Rob was at school this morning.
   No, he wasn't. He was in town.
2 Rob was in the post office.
3 Rob was in the sports shop to buy a football.
4 Rob's wallet was in his jacket.
5 Rob wants to pay for the food.

8 Everyday English

(a) How do you say these expressions from the story in your language?

1 Calm down!
2 Can I have a look?
3 Oh, brilliant!
4 You must be joking!

(b) Complete the dialogues with the expressions from Exercise 8a.

1 A: Do you want to listen to the new Natalie Imbruglia CD?

B: .... I hate her music!

2 A: I'm really worried. We've got a French test tomorrow!

B: .... It isn't a very important test.

3 A: The History teacher's ill – no History lesson today!

B: .... My project isn't ready – now I can finish it tonight!

4 A: That exercise was hard! .... at the answers now?

B: Yes, OK. They're at the back of the book.

9 Write

(a) Read the email from Harry to Maggie. Where was Harry on holiday? Was it a good holiday?

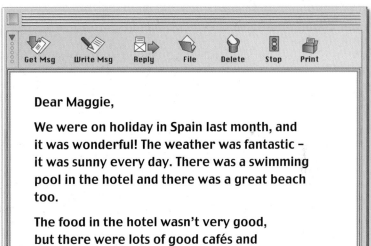

Dear Maggie,

We were on holiday in Spain last month, and it was wonderful! The weather was fantastic – it was sunny every day. There was a swimming pool in the hotel and there was a great beach too.

The food in the hotel wasn't very good, but there were lots of good cafés and restaurants in the town.

I hope we go there again next year!

Love, Harry

(b) Write an email to a friend about a holiday. Use these questions and Harry's email to help you.

- when? last year / summer / month
- weather? not good / OK / wonderful
- swimming pool or beach? great / not very nice
- hotel or restaurants? good food / not very good food

For your portfolio

14 She didn't listen

* Past simple: regular verbs, questions and negatives
* Vocabulary: verb and noun pairs

1 Read and listen

a When was the Crimean War? When was Florence Nightingale born? Read the text quickly to check your answers.

The lady with the lamp

In 1854 a war started between Britain, France and Turkey, and Russia. It was called the Crimean War. The hospitals for the soldiers were terrible. There were no beds or toilets, there was blood everywhere, the soldiers were hungry and their clothes were dirty. Many people in Britain were very angry about all this. One of them was a woman called Florence Nightingale.

Florence Nightingale was born on 12 May, 1820. When she was a girl, she studied History and Science. She was a good speaker of French, German and Italian, and she often visited other countries. Florence wanted to be a nurse, but her mother and father did not like the idea. Florence did not listen to her parents.

In October 1854, when she was 34, Florence and 37 other nurses travelled to the hospital in Scutari, in the Crimea. There was a lot of work to do, but they worked very hard. After six months the conditions in the hospital were very different. The hospital was clean, and there were toilets, clean clothes and food for the soldiers.

The soldiers at Scutari loved Florence Nightingale and called her 'The lady with the lamp'. Soon, she was famous in Britain and all over the world. She died on 13 August 1910, when she was 90.

b Read the text again and listen. Answer the questions.

1 Why were the hospitals terrible?
2 Florence wanted to be a nurse. Were her mother and father happy?
3 What was different in the Scutari hospital after six months?
4 The soldiers called Florence 'The lady with the lamp'. Why, do you think?

2 Grammar

Past simple

a Look at the examples from the text on page 98, then complete the rule.

*Florence **wanted** to be a nurse.*

*She **studied** History and Science.*

*They **travelled** to the hospital in Scutari.*

> **Rule:** To form the past simple with regular verbs, add ....
> If the verb ends in -*y*, change *y* to .... and add -*ed*.

b Match the two parts to make true sentences about the text on page 98.

Florence Nightingale	a	called her the lady with the lamp.
	b	studied History and Science.
	c	visited many hospitals in Europe.
The soldiers	d	loved Florence Nightingale.
	e	died in 1910.

Regular verbs

c Read the text below. Complete the sentences with the past simple form of the verbs in the box.

| like | ~~watch~~ | ask | want | start | like | die |
| listen | study | | | | | |

3 Pronunciation

-ed endings

a 🔊 Listen and repeat the sentences.

1 /t/   We watched a film.
2 /d/   I called a friend.
3 /ɪd/ He wanted an ice cream.

b 🔊 Listen to the verbs and repeat.

phoned	walked
visited	asked
lived	started

c 🔊 Listen again, then write the verbs from Exercise 3b in the table.

/t/	/d/	/ɪd/
....	....	....
....	....	....

I *watched* an interesting film on TV yesterday. It was about a war between England and China in the 19th century. In the war, Robin Moore, a British soldier, almost ⁱ .... A Chinese soldier, Li Fung, saved his life. Li Fung's daughter, Weili, was a nurse. She looked after Robin and she ² .... him a lot. Robin really ³ .... Weili too.

But there was one problem – language. Weili did not speak English, and Robin did not speak Chinese. Robin really ⁴ .... to understand Weili, so he ⁵ .... to learn Chinese. He stayed at Li Fung's house for five years. He ⁶ .... to Weili a lot, he ⁷ .... Chinese grammar and he ⁸ .... Weili a lot of questions. After three years, Robin's Chinese was excellent. They were both very happy.

4 Listen

a Work with a partner. Match the questions and answers.

What happened on ...

1	... 12 May 1820?	a	The first man landed on the moon.
2	... 20 July 1969?	b	The Olympic Games in Sydney ended.
3	... 15 September 2000?	c	Florence Nightingale was born.
4	... 1 October 2000?	d	John F. Kennedy died.
5	... 22 November 1963?	e	The Olympic Games in Sydney started.

b 🔊 Listen to a radio quiz show. Check your answers to Exercise 4a.

5 Grammar

Past simple: questions and negatives

a Here are three things that the people in the quiz show said. Some words are missing. Write words from the box in the spaces.

> land   did   die   didn't   did   land

1 When _____ John F. Kennedy _____ ?
2 When _____ the first man _____ on the moon?
3 Neil Armstrong _____ _____ on the moon in 1959, it was 1969.

b Look at the examples. Then complete the rules and the table.

*John F. Kennedy **didn't die** in 1945, he died in 1963.*

*When **did** Florence Nightingale **go** to Scutari?*

***Did** the Sydney Olympics **end** in 2000?*

> **Rules:** To make negatives in the past simple we use *did not*
> (............) + the base form of the verb. To make questions in the
> past simple we use .... + the base form.

Negative	Question	Short answer
I/you/he/she/we/they **didn't** (**did not**) like the film.	.... I/you/he/she/we/they like the film?	Yes, I/you/he/she/we/they **did**. No, I/you/he/she/we/they ....

c Write the negative sentences.

1 I arrived late. I *didn't arrive* late.
2 You used my computer.
  You _____ my computer.
3 We watched the film.
  We _____ .
4 She travelled to Rome. _____ .
5 They visited their grandparents.
  _____ .

d Write the questions.

1 She watched the soap opera. What *did she watch* ?
2 It happened in New York. Where _____ ?
3 They studied Latin. What _____ ?
4 I had a pizza on Saturday. When _____ ?
  _____ ?
5 We went to Italy in the summer. Where _____ ?

6 Speak

a Complete the questionnaire. Put a tick (✓) for *yes* or a cross (✗) for *no* in the 'Me' column.

	Me	My partner
1 This morning, did you		
a have a shower?	☐	☐
b have coffee for breakfast?	☐	☐
c go to school by car?	☐	☐
2 Last night, did you		
a watch TV?	☐	☐
b go to bed before 11 o'clock?	☐	☐
c study?	☐	☐
3 Last weekend, did you		
a help your parents?	☐	☐
b go to the cinema?	☐	☐
c play any sports?	☐	☐
4 Yesterday, did you		
a have an ice cream?	☐	☐
b listen to music?	☐	☐
c practise English?	☐	☐

b Work with a partner. Ask and answer the questions from Exercise 6a and fill in the 'My partner' column.

A: *Did you have coffee for breakfast this morning?*

B: *Yes, I did. Did you?*

c Work with a partner. Use question words *what*, *when*, *where* to ask and answer questions.

A: *What did you do last night?*

B: *I studied English.*

A: *Did you? I watched a film on TV. Where did you ... ?*

7 Vocabulary

Verb and noun pairs

a Match the verbs and the nouns. Write the nouns in four lists. Use the questionnaire in Exercise 6a to help you.

> a shower   bed   a coffee   (an) ice cream   school
> sports   the cinema   English

have	practise	play	go to
a shower			

b Now put these nouns in the four lists in Exercise 7a.

> the piano (x2)   work   breakfast/lunch/dinner   a party (x2)
> a bath

Culture in mind

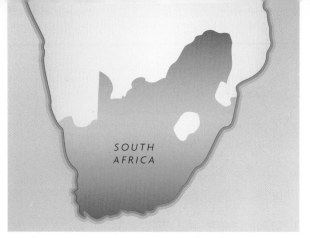

SOUTH
AFRICA

8 Read

(a) Look at the photos. What do you know about South Africa? What was apartheid? Read the article and check your ideas.

South Africa: population 43,000,000.
Black: 75%; white: 13%; others: 12%

STEVE BIKO

A SOUTH AFRICAN HERO

STEVE BIKO

For over 100 years, the country of South Africa had a system called 'apartheid'. Apartheid separated black and white people. It meant that black people in South Africa could not vote or go to the same places as white people. They could not live in the same places, and they could not get many of the jobs that white people had. Black South Africans, and many white South Africans too, hated this system, and they tried for many years to change it. One of these people was Steve Biko.

Steve Biko was born in 1946 in King Williams Town in South Africa, and he studied Medicine at university. In the 1960s he was one of the leaders of a student group that worked against apartheid in South Africa. In 1969, he was the first president of the South African Students' Organisation. He worked hard to help black people in his country, and in 1972 he became president of the Black People's Convention. The white South African government didn't like Biko, and he went to prison many times. In 1977, the police took him to prison again, and this time he didn't come out. The police beat him, and he died in a prison hospital in Port Elizabeth. Steve Biko was only 31 years old.

Fourteen years later, in 1991, apartheid ended and in 1994, Nelson Mandela became the first black president of South Africa.

NELSON MANDELA

b Read the article again and mark the statements *T* (true) or *F* (false).

1 Because of apartheid, black people could not do many things that white people could do. □
2 All white South African people liked apartheid. □
3 Steve Biko studied to be a doctor. □
4 Biko was president of an organisation that worked against apartheid. □
5 Biko first went to prison in August 1977. □
6 Apartheid ended in South Africa in 1988. □
7 Steve Biko was the first black president of South Africa. □

c Why do you think there was apartheid in South Africa?

9 Write

a Read Beth's article for the school magazine.

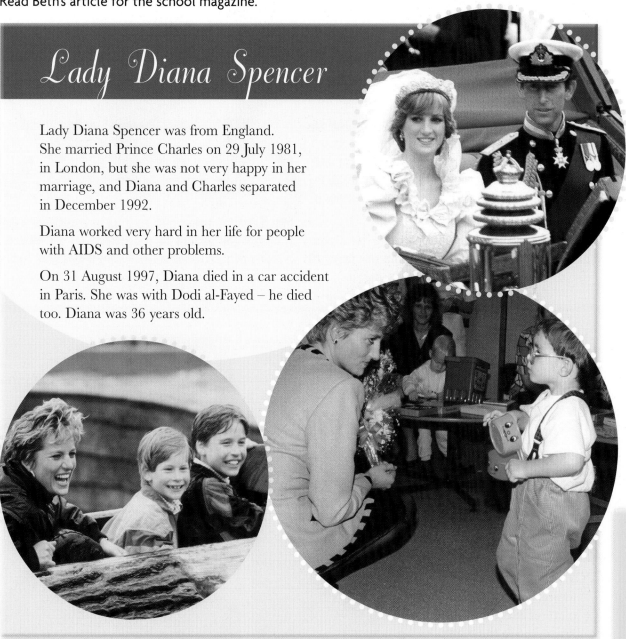

Lady Diana Spencer

Lady Diana Spencer was from England. She married Prince Charles on 29 July 1981, in London, but she was not very happy in her marriage, and Diana and Charles separated in December 1992.

Diana worked very hard in her life for people with AIDS and other problems.

On 31 August 1997, Diana died in a car accident in Paris. She was with Dodi al-Fayed – he died too. Diana was 36 years old.

b Write a paragraph about a famous person for your school magazine. Use the texts about Steve Biko and Lady Diana Spencer to help you.

For your portfolio

15 Where did they go?

* Past simple: irregular verbs
* Vocabulary: adverbs

1 Read and listen

a Look at the photo and the title of the article. What do you think the mystery is about?

1 a man who won the lottery
2 a man who stole a lot of money from a bank
3 a man who disappeared

b Read the article quickly to check your ideas.

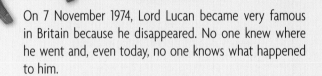

The mystery of Lord Lucan

Lord 'Lucky' Lucan was a rich, good-looking man. He was married with three children. He had an expensive house in London, and he loved gambling on horse races and in the London casinos. People called him 'Lucky' because they thought he had a good life and it seemed he didn't have any problems.

But in the early 1970s, Lord Lucan started to lose a lot of money with his gambling, and he and his wife began to live apart.

On 7 November 1974, Lord Lucan became very famous in Britain because he disappeared. No one knew where he went and, even today, no one knows what happened to him.

c 🔊 Read the text again and listen. Answer the questions.

1 What did Lord Lucan like doing with his money?
2 What happened in the early 1970s?
3 Do we know where Lord Lucan went in 1974?
4 Do we know where Lord Lucan is now?

a

b

c

d

e

f

2 Listen

a 🔊 Listen to the radio interview and put the pictures in the correct order. Write 2–6 in the boxes.

b What do you think happened to Lord Lucan?

3 Grammar

Past simple: irregular verbs

a Look at these examples. <u>Underline</u> examples of past simple irregular verbs in the article on page 104. Then complete the table. Use the irregular verb list on page 122 to help you.

*He **had** an expensive house in London.*
*No one **knew** where he **went**.*

become	*became*	run (away)	....	take	....
find	....	say	....	tell	....
get	....	see	....	think	....
go	....	speak	....	wake (up)	....

b Complete the sentences with the correct forms of the verb.

1 Tom: I ___*wrote*___ a thank-you letter to Aunt Jane yesterday. (write)

   Mum: Good. _____ you _____ to Grandma, too?

2 Mary: _____ you _____ Jenny last night? (see)

   Martin: No, but I _____ Steve. He wasn't very well.

3 Sue: _____ you _____ to Scotland by train? (go)

   Javed: No, the train's very slow. We _____ by plane this time.

4 Maria: _____ you _____ a lot of presents for your birthday? (get)

   Jon: Yes, and I _____ a new bike from my parents!

c Put the words in the box in the past simple. Then use these words to complete the paragraph about Agatha Christie.

~~be~~	have	know
speak	write	
go	become	

Agatha Christie ___*was*___ born in Devon in 1890. She ¹_____ over sixty detective novels, and ²_____ very famous. Her books are still popular today. She got married in 1914 and ³_____ a daughter, Rosalind. In 1926, Agatha disappeared for ten days. No one ⁴_____ where she ⁵_____ . She died in 1976, but she never ⁶_____ about her mysterious disappearance.

4 Speak

a Work with a partner. Number the pictures 1–6 to make a story.

run to school

get dressed

have a shower

get back home / see clock / 7.05!

Tom / wake up late

arrive at school / no one there!

b Tell the story. Use the verbs below the pictures in the past simple.

5 Read

a Read the text and answer the questions.

1 When did the people go on board the ship?
2 Why were there no signals from the crew of the *Mary Celeste*?
3 How many people were on the *Mary Celeste* when she left New York?
4 How do we know the crew left quickly?

A mystery at sea

It was the afternoon of December 5, 1872, and a ship called the *Dei Gratia* was near the coast of Portugal. Suddenly, the Captain (Captain Morehouse) saw another small ship. It looked out of control, but there were no signals from the crew. After two hours, a group of people went on board the ship. What they saw was very strange.

A ship like this was normally noisy and busy, but the *Mary Celeste* was completely silent. Captain Briggs, his wife Sarah, two-year-old daughter Sophia Matilda, and the crew of seven were nowhere on board.

The crew probably left very quickly, because there were cups of tea and food on the tables. The ship's cat was still there, but there were no people.

The ship was the *Mary Celeste* from New York. Her story is still one of the great mysteries of the sea. Did the Captain think there was a danger on board? Did he suddenly see an iceberg? Maybe there was a storm at sea? Or perhaps there was even a sea monster?

All we know for sure is that no one ever saw the captain and crew of the *Mary Celeste* again.

b What do you think happened to the *Mary Celeste*?

6 Vocabulary

Adverbs

a Look at the examples. Then complete the rule.

*Suddenly, the Captain **saw** another small ship.*

*The crew probably **left** very quickly.*

> **Rule:** Adverbs often describe verbs. To form regular adverbs, we usually add .... to the adjective. If the adjective ends in a *y* change the *y* to *i* and add **-ly**.

b Put the adjectives in the box into adverbs. Then complete the sentences with the correct adverbs.

> ~~quiet~~ angry slow quick sudden careful bad

1 Maria speaks so ....*quietly*...., I can't hear her.

2 I write very .... I wrote only 100 words in three hours!

3 Tom and Alicia work very .... They finished all their homework in 20 minutes!

4 In an exam, you need to read the questions very .... before you answer them.

5 Our football team played very .... We lost 4–0!

6 The car came round the corner very .... I didn't see it, so I fell off my bike.

7 Jack's parents shouted at him .... when he arrived home late.

7 Pronunciation

Adverbs

🔊 Listen and repeat.

1	quietly	4	quickly	6	slowly
2	suddenly	5	carefully	7	angrily
3	probably				

8 Speak

a Look at the examples from the text on page 106. When do we use *maybe* and *perhaps*? When do we use *probably*?

Maybe there was a storm at sea.
*The crew **probably** left very quickly.*
Perhaps there was even a sea monster.

b Work with a partner. What do you think happened to the *Mary Celeste*? Make guesses. Use the language in Exercise 8a.

A: *Maybe a sea monster killed them.*
B: *No, I don't think that's true! I think they **probably** …*

c Look at the pictures. What do they show? Make guesses.

①

②

③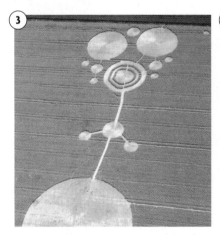

④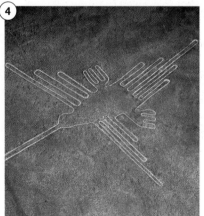

A: *What's picture 1, do you think?*
B: *Perhaps it's a UFO.*
A: *Or maybe it isn't a real photo. I think it's probably a ….*

Who's Caroline?

9 Read and listen

(a) 🔊 Look at the title of the photo story and the pictures. What happened, do you think?
Read, listen and check your answer.

1

Alex: Like my new coat, Mum? I bought it today.
Mum: Yes, it's really smart.

2

Alex: There's something in the pocket. It's a photograph.

3

Mum: She's pretty! It says 'To Alex, all my love, Caroline'. Who's Caroline?
Alex: No idea!
Mum: Is she your girlfriend, Alex?
Alex: No, Mum! Honestly, I don't know her. It's a real mystery to me.

A week later ...

4

Boy: I brought a coat back last week. It had a hole in it.
Shop Assistant: Yes, I remember.
Boy: Did you find a photograph in the pocket?
Shop Assistant: No, sorry.

5

Alex: But I did! Is your name Alex, too?
Boy: That's right. Oh great! Thanks a lot! And there's a hole in that coat!
Alex: Why did you sell me a coat with a hole in it?

b Write the missing verbs in the past simple in the spaces.

Alex __bought__ (buy) a new coat. He [1]_____ (go) home and [2]_____ (show) it to his mum. Then he [3]_____ (find) a photograph of a girl in the pocket. His mum [4]_____ (think) that the girl was Alex's girlfriend, but he [5]_____ (have) no idea who she was. Alex [6]_____ (go) back to the shop. There [7]_____ (be) a boy in the shop who [8]_____ (ask) the shop assistant about the photograph. Alex [9]_____ (give) the photograph to the boy. The boy [10]_____ (say) 'Thanks a lot' and showed Alex a hole in his coat. Alex [11]_____ (be) very angry with the shop assistant.

10 Everyday English

a Find these two expressions in the story on page 108. Who says them?

1 Like my new coat?
2 No idea.

Sometimes you hear English speakers ask questions like:

Want an ice cream?
Happy?
Got a problem?

The complete questions are:

***Do** you want an ice cream?*
***Are** you happy?*
***Have** you got a problem?*

b Look again at expressions 1 and 2 in Exercise 10a. What are the complete questions?

c Read the short conversations. What are the complete questions?

1 Tony: Hungry?
   Chris: Yeah.
   Tony: Want to have lunch?

2 Didem: Got a minute?
   Esra: Yes, what's wrong?
   Didem: There's a problem with my computer.
   Esra: Want me to help you?

11 Write

a Read Josh's letter to his friend and answer the questions.

1 Where did Josh visit?
2 What was it like inside?
3 Who was his guide?
4 What happened to the guide?

Dear Sam

I visited this castle yesterday, and it was really strange. It was very dark and it felt cold inside. The guide was a tall man with very long arms and legs. When he told me about the castle, he spoke very quietly. Then I went into the little shop for this photo. When I came out, the man wasn't there. I asked the woman in the shop and she said 'The castle guide isn't here any more. He disappeared last winter.' After that, I left very quickly! Perhaps the man was a ghost! What do you think?!

Love Josh

b Now write a story about a strange place you visited. Use Josh's letter and the words in the box to help you.

old house   empty rooms   strange woman
table with food and drinks

For your portfolio

16 Now and then

* Comparison of adjectives
* *than*
* Vocabulary: adjectives and opposites

1 Listen

(a) Look at the photographs of London in the 1950s, and London in the early 21st century. What things are different, and what things are the same?

(b) 🔊 Listen to Lucy and her grandfather. They talk about life in the 1950s and life now. Who talks about these things? Write G (grandfather) or L (Lucy).

Is life better now❓

1   The streets in the town ☐
2   School life ☐
3   DVDs ☐ G
4   The shops ☐
5   Television ☐
6   Mobile phones ☐

(c) Listen again. Mark the sentences *T* (true) or *F* (false).

1   Lucy's grandfather thinks life is better now than in the 1950s. ☐
2   He didn't watch television when he was young. ☐
3   He thinks Lucy's life at school is easy. ☐
4   Lucy says it is easy for her grandfather to walk in the streets. ☐
5   Lucy says her grandfather is a happy man. ☐

2 Grammar

Comparison of adjectives

a 🔊 Who said these sentences in the conversation? Write *G* (grandfather) or *L* (Lucy) in the boxes. Then listen again and check your answers.

1 Life was good for me when I was younger. `G`
2 Now he's older. ☐
3 Some things are easier now. ☐
4 Perhaps she's happier than I was. ☐
5 School life is more difficult now. ☐
6 Life is more interesting now. ☐
7 Yes, life was good. Is it better now? ☐
8 Perhaps life is worse for him now. ☐

b Complete the table and the rule. Use the examples in Exercise 2a to help you.

Adjective	Comparative adjective
old big young	*older* bigger ....
easy happy	*easier* ....
difficult interesting	.... difficult .... interesting
good bad	....

> **Rule:**
> - short adjectives: we usually add *-er* .
>   If the adjective ends in *y*, change the *y*
>   to .... If it ends in vowel + consonant,
>   double the consonant (e.g. *big → bigger*)
> - longer adjectives: add the word ....
>   before the adjective
> - irregular adjectives: use a different word:
>   good – *better*; bad – ....

c Write the comparative adjectives for these adjectives.

1 near ....
2 tall ....
3 cheap ....
4 funny ....
5 important ....
6 fast ....
7 expensive ....
8 hot ....

d Complete the sentences. Use the correct forms of the adjectives.

1 Rio's ...... *hot* ...... , but Delhi's
   ...... *hotter* .... (hot)
2 Trains are .... , but planes are
   .... (fast)
3 Mike's joke was .... , but Annie's
   joke was .... (funny)
4 Haytown's .... , but Moreton's
   .... (near)
5 The Grand Hotel's very .... ,
   but the Plaza Hotel's ....
   (expensive)
6 Matt's really .... , but Andy's
   even .... ! (tall)

than

e Look at the examples from the listening on page 110.

*I was **freer than** her.*
*... she's **happier than** I was.*

f Rewrite the sentences in Exercise 2d.

*Delhi's **hotter than** Rio.*

3 Pronunciation

/ðən/ than

a 🔊 Listen. How is *than* pronounced?

1 She's taller than me.
2 I'm older than him.
3 It's hotter than yesterday.
4 Our dog's bigger than yours.
5 This is more expensive than that one.

b 🔊 Listen again and repeat.

4 Speak

Compare some things / people in your classroom.

I'm older than Juan. Sandra's taller than me.
My desk's closer to the door than Mandy's
desk. ....

5 Read

a Look at the photos and the newspaper article. What does the man do? Where does he live? Where is he from? Read the article and check your answers.

Island chef cooks in LA

Jefferson Sinclair, 26, was born in Tobermory on the Scottish island of Mull. His first job was in a small café there. At the age of 22, he left Mull and travelled round the world. Now, four years later, he is living in L.A. (Los Angeles) and is the chef in a famous restaurant. Jefferson is back in Scotland for a holiday. The *Mull Times* spoke to him.

'L.A. is great!' says Jefferson. 'It's more modern and exciting than a lot of the other places I saw on my trips around the world. There are more things to do here.' Jefferson is the top chef at The Diner, a popular restaurant in Los Angeles. Does Jefferson miss the island of Mull? He smiles, 'I do. There are a lot of things I miss. Los Angeles is an exciting place, but it's noisier than Mull – there are more cars and the streets are busier. And of course, it's more dangerous than other places. Mull's safer and quieter, but it's more boring, too.'

So does he want to return to Mull? 'Well, perhaps when I'm older!' he says. 'I really enjoy my job here in L.A., and of course I earn more money here.' We wish him good luck!

b Answer the questions.

1 What was Jefferson's first job?
2 What does he miss about Mull?
3 What does he like about Los Angeles?
4 Does he want to return to Mull? Why / Why not?

6 Vocabulary

Adjectives

(a) Look at the examples from the article on page 112. Which one is about Mull?

1 It's more **modern** and **exciting**.
2 It's **noisier** ... the streets are **busier**.
3 It's **safer** and **quieter**.

(b) Write the words under the pictures.

~~dangerous~~   boring   exciting   modern   noisy   old-fashioned   quiet   safe

1 a *dangerous* street

2 a _____ place

3 a _____ disco

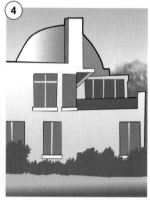

4 a _____ house

5 an _____ car

6 a _____ game

7 an _____ film

8 a _____ garden

(c) Put the words in Exercise 6b in pairs with their opposites. Write the words in the spaces.

1 exciting _____
2 dangerous _____
3 noisy _____
4 modern _____

(b) Work with a partner. Use the topics in the box to make comparisons.

A: *Snowboarding is a dangerous sport.*
B: *Yes, it is – but skiing is more dangerous than snowboarding.*

a sport
a film
a school subject
a place in your town
a text in this book
a television programme
a city in your country
a type of transport (car, train, etc.)

7 Speak

(a) Work with a partner. Talk about things in your life. Use the adjectives in Exercise 6.

A: *Our house is modern, but I like old-fashioned houses.*
B: *Really? I like modern houses.*
A: *Our town is boring. There aren't any ...*

Culture in mind

8 Read

a Look at the photos. What is a 'holiday camp'? How do you think holiday camps in the 1950s were different from today's?

b Read the magazine article to check your answers.

UK holiday camps
then and now

Butlin's Holiday

A 1950s dream

In the 1950s, many people in the UK wanted to escape from life in the cities and enjoy a holiday at the seaside or in the countryside. This is when Butlin's holiday camps became very popular.

Life in the camps was fun, and very organised. Men and women in red coats made sure that everyone was happy. They organised games for the children, and for the adults there were shows, dances and competitions.

The camps were never quiet – happy announcements on the public loudspeaker system started at 6.30 in the morning to tell people to come for breakfast. There were more messages during the day. And when there weren't any messages, there was non-stop music.

Center Parcs

Today's luxury holiday

Center Parcs today are popular with millions of British people. But of course Center Parcs are different from Butlin's holiday camps. They are bigger, quieter and more comfortable than Butlin's camps were. But they are also more expensive. And they are less organised – people can do what they want, and there are more things for people to do.

Center Parcs are in beautiful villages with luxury villas and lots of sports facilities. You can go riding or climbing, play golf, or go canoeing or swimming. There is also the 'subtropical swimming paradise'. This is a big glass building, and inside, the temperature is always between 25 and 30°C. There are palm trees, little rivers and pools. There are also outside pools with seats and tables in them. At night, people sit by the pools, enjoy dinner, and look at the stars.

(c) Mark the statements *T* (true) or *F* (false).

1   More than 50 years ago, many British people started to like Butlin's holiday camps. ☐

2   At Butlin's, men and women organised fun activities for children and adults. ☐

3   The camps were very quiet places. ☐

4   Butlin's camps were cheaper than Center Parcs. ☐

5   In Center Parcs, people can do lots of sports. ☐

6   In Center Parcs, the temperature is always between 25 and 30°C. ☐

9 Write

(a) Look at the advertisement for a competition. How much money can you win? How many words must you write?

COMPETITION!

Do you want the chance to win **500 Euros** for your school?
Enter our competition!

Either: **A**   Write a short text to compare your life now to your life as it was six years ago.

Or: **B**   Write a short text to compare life as it was 100 years ago to life as it is now.

Write no more than 120 words!

(b) Read Claudia's entry. Which option did she write about, A or B?

Is my life better now, or was it better six years ago?

I think my life is better now. I've got more friends now than I had six years ago. I'm older, so I can do more interesting things. I can go to the cinema, I can go out with friends, and I can go to bed later in the evenings. I've got my own room, and lots of CDs and books. Six years ago, I didn't have a mobile phone or a laptop and email.

What are the things about my life now that I don't like? I've got more things to do, at home and at school. School is more difficult, and I think my life is busier.

(c) Write your entry for the competition. Choose option A or B. Use Claudia's model to help you organise your answer.

For your portfolio

Module 4 **Check your progress**

1 **Grammar**

a Complete the dialogue with the past simple form of *be*.

A: You _weren't_ at school last week. Where ¹_____ you?

B: I ²_____ at home, in bed.

A: Oh, what ³_____ the matter with you? ⁴_____ you tired?

B: No, I ⁵_____ very well. My parents ⁶_____ worried.

A: I'm sure they ⁷_____! Well, the lessons ⁸_____ very interesting.

B: Oh good. [8]

b Complete the sentences. Use the past simple form of the verbs.

Last night we _watched_ (watch) a programme on TV. It ¹_____ (tell) the story of a famous man from India called Mahatma Gandhi. Gandhi ²_____ (live) in South Africa when he was young, but in 1914 he ³_____ (go) back to India. Gandhi ⁴_____ (become) very famous there because he ⁵_____ (think) fighting was bad. In 1947, the British ⁶_____ (leave) India, but Gandhi ⁷_____ (die) the next year. We ⁸_____ (find) the programme very interesting and I ⁹_____ (learn) a lot. [9]

c Write the questions.

1 A: I found your pen.
   B: Great! Where _did_ you _find_ it?

2 A: I went to France last year.
   B: Really? _____ you _____ to Paris?

3 A: Yes. We saw the Eiffel Tower.
   B: _____ you _____ the Louvre too?

4 A: I spoke French all the time.
   B: _____ your parents _____ French too?

5 A: I understood everything!
   B: OK – but _____ people _____ you? [4]

d Complete the sentences. Use the past simple forms of the verbs.

1 We _went_ (go) to the cinema last week, but we _didn't go_ (not go) shopping.

2 I _____ (write) six emails yesterday, but I _____ (not write) any letters.

3 Alan _____ (come) to the party, but Peter _____ (not come).

4 I _____ (eat) the chips, but I _____ (not eat) the carrots!

5 We _____ (see) Mark last night, but we _____ (not see) his brother. [4]

e Complete the sentences. Use the comparative form of the adjectives.

1 Ella's hair is _longer_ (long) than Petra's.

2 Yesterday was _____ (hot) than today.

3 Sheila finds Spanish _____ (easy) than Dutch.

4 His first book was _____ (funny) than his new one.

5 Are you _____ (happy) now than when you were a little child? [4]

f Write comparative sentences.

1 this test / difficult / the Maths test
   This test is more difficult than the Maths test.

2 my uncle's car / expensive / my father's
   _____

3 your homework / important / that computer game
   _____

4 her History teacher / good / my teacher
   _____

5 the weather in winter / bad / in summer
   _____ [4]

2 Vocabulary

(a) Match the dates with the numbers.

1	the seventeenth of September nineteen forty-one	a	14.11.2003
2	the third of August nineteen eighty-eight	b	22.02.1999
3	the twenty-second of February nineteen ninety-nine	c	31.12.2000
4	the fourteenth of November two thousand and three	d	17.09.1941
5	the second of May nineteen seventy-six	e	02.05.1976
6	the thirty-first of December two thousand	f	03.08.1988

5

(b) Underline the correct word.

1 She went into the room *quiet/quietly* but the baby woke up.

2 I slept *bad/badly* because the bed was very small.

3 My grandmother was *angry/angrily* when her computer stopped.

4 He made the cake *careful/carefully* and it won the competition.

5 Don't drive so *slow/slowly* – we're late!

6 He speaks Italian very *good/well* because he was born in Milan.

7 They worked *quick/quickly* and finished before bedtime.

8 The car stopped *sudden/suddenly* when a cat ran in front of it.

7

(c) Write the nouns in the box in the lists.

a bath   work   a look   the piano
tennis   cards   the cinema   an ice cream
football   bed   school   a cup of tea

have	play	go to
a bath	*tennis*	*school*

9

3 Everyday English

Complete the dialogues with the expressions in the box.

Calm down   Can I have a look
Oh, brilliant   Got a problem
You must be joking

Anna: It's no good! I can't do it!

Marek: [1] *Got a problem* ?

Anna: Yes, I have! A big one. I can't do this and I've got a test tomorrow!

Marek: [2] _____ , Annie!

Anna: But I don't understand the question.

Marek: [3] _____ ?

Anna: OK. It's this one, here.

Marek: That's really easy.

Anna: [4] _____ ! It's impossible!

Marek: No, it's easy. The answer is f.

Anna: [5] _____ , Marek. Thanks!

4

How did you do?

Tick (✓) a box for each section.

Total score 58	☺ Very good	☺ OK	☹ Not very good
Grammar	24 – 33	19 – 23	less than 19
Vocabulary	16 – 21	13 – 15	less than 13
Everyday English	3 – 4	2	less than 2

Project 1
A group presentation

Our favourite band:

COLDPLAY

Coldplay are a British band. They are four men: Chris Martin, Guy Berryman, Jonny Buckland, and Will Champion.

Chris Martin is from Devon and he sings, and plays the guitar and piano. Guy Berryman is from Scotland and he plays the bass guitar. Jonny Buckland is from Wales and he plays the lead guitar. Will Champion is from Southampton and he plays the drums. They are all about 28 years old.

Coldplay are very successful and their music is great! They have a lot of brilliant CDs, for example Parachutes and A rush of blood to the head. Our favourite songs are Shiver, Yellow, and Brothers and Sisters.

1 Do your research

(a) Work in groups of three or four. Choose a singer or a band your group likes. Collect information about the band. Use these questions to help you:

- What's the singer's or band's name?
- Where is he/she from? Where are they from?
- How old are they?
- What instruments do they play?
- What are your favourite songs or albums?

(b) Write a short text about the singer or band. Use the example and the questions in Exercise 1a to help you.

(c) Collect pictures. Get a large piece of paper or card for your poster. Stick the pictures on poster paper and add your texts.

(d) Get a song by the singer or band that you like.

2 Prepare the presentation

(a) Practise presenting your poster. Read your texts aloud.

(b) Present your poster to another group or the class. At the end of your presentation, play a song if you want to.

For your portfolio

Project 2
A tourist leaflet

1 Do your research

a Work in groups of three or four. Choose a town or city. Get some facts about the town or city and write notes. Use these questions and the example to help you:

- What kinds of shops are there in your town/city?
- What interesting places are there for tourists? (For example, museums, markets, cafés/restaurants.)
- Are there interesting places near your town/city?
- Why is your town/city special?

b Collect photos or draw pictures of your town/city.

Make the leaflet

a Get a large piece of paper. Ask your teacher to show you how to fold it.

b Write your information. Use these ideas and the example on this page to help you:

- On the front cover page, write *Come and visit* and add the name of your town or city. Add a picture of an interesting place in your town/city.
- On pages 1 and 2, draw a map of your town/city or a part of it. Write names to the places and streets.
- On pages 3–6, add pictures of places in your town/city and write your information.

c If you have time, write a quiz about your town/city.

Old Town (Stare Miasto)

Park (Planty)

map of Kraków

Cloth Hall (Sukiennice)

Old Town Square (Rynek Główny)

Park (planty)

Wawel

Wisła River

COME AND VISIT Kraków!

Kraków is the old capital of Poland.

There are a lot of things to see and do in Kraków! Try these.

Visit the beautiful Old Town (Stare Miasto), and go to the Main Market Square (Rynek Główny). See the wonderful old clock there, or sit in a café and watch the people.

Do you like shopping? Visit the Cloth Hall (Sukiennice). There are a lot of things to buy there! For example, Polish crafts from the market to take home with you.

Do you want to relax? Walk in the park (planty) around the Old Town!

Do you like old buildings? Visit Wawel Hill and see Kraków from the top. Go to Wawel Royal Castle (Zamek Królewski) and see the dragon's den.

Project 3
A survey about free time

1 Prepare the survey

a Work in groups of three or four. Choose one topic about free time. Use these topic ideas to help you:

- music
- sports
- TV
- shopping
- food

b Together, write four or five questions to ask other students in the class. Use the example to help you.

Sports

Name   Barbara

1   What kinds of sports do you like?   *Likes tennis and football.*

2   How often do you play sports?   ....

3   Who's your favourite football team?   ....

4   Do you like watching sports on TV?   ....

5   Can you .... ?   ....

c Each student in your group asks two or three students from another group and takes notes.

2 Write the report

a Work in your group. Tell the other students your information. Write the results on one piece of paper.

Barbara likes tennis and football. She doesn't play football, she watches it on TV. Her favourite team is ...

b In your group, write a report and present your work to the class.

Three people in our class play football after school. Two boys and one girl.

All the boys in our survey like watching sports on TV, but only three girls like watching sports on TV ...

For your portfolio

Project 4

A presentation on changes in your country

1 Do your research

a) Work in groups of three or four. In your group, choose one or two topics you would like to focus on. Look at these topic ideas to help you:

- town/city life (shopping, streets, buildings, roads and transport)
- school life
- free time activities (sports, cinema, theatre, TV, etc.)
- food and eating out
- family and home life

b) What do you want to find out about the past? How are things different now? Write some questions to help you get information. Look at these example questions:

Family and home life

- Were families bigger or smaller in your country 50 years ago?
- Did young people get married and leave home later or earlier than they do now?
- Did old people usually live with their families?
- Were houses smaller than they are now? Did children share their bedrooms?

c) Talk to older people you know, from your country, for example grandparents. Ask them how things were 50 years ago, and how things are different now. Write down their answers, or record them on a cassette player.

d) Find more information about your country as it was 50 years ago. Look on the Internet, or in a library or museum. Try to get some photos of your country 50 years ago.

2 Do the presentation

a) In your group, organise the information you have. You can present your information on a large piece of paper or card. Write your information and add any photos you have.

b) Take it in turns to present your information. If you can, use photographs to illustrate your presentation. First, tell your class what your presentation is about.

This presentation is about family and home life in our country 50 years ago, compared to today. In the 1950s, families in ... were ... than today ...

For your portfolio

✱ Irregular verbs and phonetics

Irregular verbs

Base form	Past simple
be	was/were
beat	beat
become	became
begin	began
bite	bit
break	broke
build	built
buy	bought
can	could
catch	caught
choose	chose
come	came
cut	cut
do	did
drive	drove
eat	ate
fall	fell
feel	felt
find	found
fly	flew
get	got
give	gave
go	went
grow	grew
have	had
hear	heard
hit	hit
hurt	hurt
keep	kept
know	knew
leave	left
lose	lost
make	made
meet	met
put	put
read	read
ride	rode
run	ran
say	said
see	saw
sell	sold
send	sent
sit	sat
sleep	slept
speak	spoke
stand	stood
swim	swam
take	took
teach	taught
tell	told
think	thought
throw	threw
understand	understood
wake	woke
win	won
write	wrote

Phonetic symbols

Consonants

/p/	pen
/b/	be
/t/	two
/d/	do
/k/	can
/g/	good
/f/	five
/v/	very
/m/	make
/n/	nice
/ŋ/	sing
/s/	see
/z/	trousers
/w/	we
/l/	listen
/r/	right
/j/	you
/h/	he
/θ/	thing
/ð/	this
/ʃ/	she
/tʃ/	cheese
/ʒ/	usually
/dʒ/	German

Vowels

/æ/	man
/ɑː/	father
/e/	ten
/ɜː/	thirteen
/ə/	mother
/ɪ/	sit
/iː/	see
/ʊ/	book
/uː/	food
/ʌ/	up
/ɒ/	hot
/ɔː/	four

Diphthongs

/eɪ/	great
/aɪ/	fine
/ɔɪ/	boy
/ɪə/	hear
/eə/	chair
/aʊ/	town
/əʊ/	go
/ʊə/	pure

Wordlist

(v) = verb   (n) = noun   (adj) = adjective   (adv) = adverb

Unit 1

Classroom objects

board (n) /bɔːd/
book (n) /bʊk/
cassette (n) /kə'set/
chair (n) /tʃeəʳ/
desk (n) /desk/
notebook (n) /'nəʊtbʊk/
pen (n) /pen/
pencil (n) /'pensəl/

People

man (n) /mæn/
men (n) /men/
people (n) /'piːpl/
person (n) /'pɜːsən/
woman (n) /'wʊmən/
women (n) /'wɪmɪn/

Verbs

can /kæn/
know /nəʊ/
open /'əʊpən/
read /riːd/

Nouns

answer /'ɑːnsəʳ/
CD /,siː'diː/
cinema /'sɪnəmə/
city /'sɪti/
computer /kəm'pjuːtəʳ/
computer game
    /kəm'pjuːtəʳ geɪm/
door /dɔːʳ/
film /fɪlm/
football /'fʊtbɔːl/
football team /'fʊtbɔːl
    tiːm/
hamburger /'hæm,bɜːgəʳ/
homework /'həʊmwɜːk/
hotel /həʊ'tel/
message /'mesɪdʒ/
museum /mjuː'ziːəm/
name /neɪm/
page /peɪdʒ/
phone /fəʊn/
pizza /'piːtsə/
restaurant /'restərɒnt/
sandwich /'sænwɪdʒ/
singer /'sɪŋəʳ/
taxi /'tæksi/
teacher /'tiːtʃəʳ/
TV /,tiː'viː/
video /'vɪdiəʊ/
window /'wɪndəʊ/

Adjectives

bad /bæd/
big /bɪg/
boring /'bɔːrɪŋ/
cheap /tʃiːp/
correct /kə'rekt/
excellent /'eksələnt/
expensive /ɪk'spensɪv/
good /gʊd/
interesting /'ɪntrəstɪŋ/
new /njuː/
old /əʊld/
small /smɔːl/

Question words

what /wɒt/

Prepositions

from /frɒm/
in /ɪn/
on /ɒn/

Everyday English

Excellent. /'eksələnt/
I can help you. /aɪ kən
    help juː/
I don't understand. /aɪ
    dəʊnt ,ʌndə'stænd/
I know. /aɪ nəʊ/
No problem. /nəʊ
    'prɒbləm/
OK? /əʊ'keɪ/
Sorry, I don't know. /'sɒri aɪ
    dəʊnt nəʊ/
Thanks. /θæŋks/
That's correct. /ðæts
    kə'rekt/
What's the answer? /wɒts
    ðiː 'ɑːnsəʳ/
Yes, great. /jes greɪt/

Unit 2

Countries

Argentina (n) /,ɑːdʒən'tiːnə/
Belgium (n) /'beldʒəm/
Brazil (n) /brə'zɪl/
Britain (n) /'brɪtən/
Canada (n) /'kænədə/
China (n) /'tʃaɪnə/
England (n) /'ɪŋglənd/
Germany (n) /'dʒɜːməni/
Italy (n) /'ɪtəli/

Japan (n) /dʒə'pæn/
Norway (n) /'nɔːweɪ/
Poland (n) /'pəʊlənd/
Portugal (n) /'pɔːtʃəgəl/
Russia (n) /'rʌʃə/
Spain (n) /speɪn/
Switzerland (n)
    /'swɪtsələnd/
Turkey (n) /'tɜːki/

Nationalities

American (adj) /ə'merɪkən/
Argentinian (adj)
    /,ɑːdʒən'tɪniən/
Australian (adj)
    /ɒs'treɪliən/
Belgian (adj) /'beldʒən/
Brazilian (adj) /brə'zɪliən/
British (adj) /'brɪtɪʃ/
Chinese (adj) /tʃaɪ'niːz/
English (adj) /'ɪŋglɪʃ/
French (adj) /frenʃ/
Irish (adj) /'aɪərɪʃ/
Italian (adj) /ɪ'tæliən/
Polish (adj) /'pəʊlɪʃ/
Spanish (adj) /'spænɪʃ/
Swedish (adj) /'swiːdɪʃ/
Turkish (adj) /'tɜːkɪʃ/

Verbs

be /biː/
think /θɪŋk/

Nouns

actor /'æktəʳ/
address /ə'dres/
best friend /best frend/
father /'fɑːðəʳ/
flag /flæg/
film star /fɪlm stɑːʳ/
footballer /'fʊtbɔːləʳ/
friend /frend/
girl /gɜːl/
golfer /'gɒlfəʳ/
hero /'hɪərəʊ/
heroine /'herəʊɪn/
mobile phone /'məʊbaɪl
    fəʊn/
model /'mɒdəl/
mother /'mʌðəʳ/
player /'pleɪəʳ/
school /skuːl/
star /stɑːʳ/
tennis /'tenɪs/
winner /'wɪnəʳ/

Adjectives

great /greɪt/
right /raɪt/

Question words

How (old) /haʊ/
What /wɒt/
Where /weəʳ/
Who /huː/

Unit 3

Verbs

come /kʌm/
go /gəʊ/
like /laɪk/
love /lʌv/
play /pleɪ/
say /seɪ/
see /siː/
want /wɒnt/

Nouns

band /bænd/
capital /'kæpɪtəl/
car /kɑːʳ/
cat /kæt/
chocolate /'tʃɒkələt/
coffee /'kɒfi/
concert /'kɒnsət/
dog /dɒg/
horse /hɔːs/
jam /dʒæm/
music /'mjuːzɪk/
pop group /pɒp gruːp/
rap /ræp/
song /sɒŋ/
speaker /'spiːkəʳ/
sport /spɔːt/
volleyball /'vɒlibɔːl/

Adjectives

awful /'ɔːfəl/
classical /'klæsɪkəl/
fantastic /fæn'tæstɪk/
favourite /'feɪvərɪt/
lucky /'lʌki/
popular /'pɒpjələʳ/
terrible /'terəbl/
wonderful /'wʌndəfəl/

Prepositions

about /əˈbaʊt/
at /æt/
of /ɒv/
with /wɪð/

Question words

How (many) /haʊ/

Everyday English

Guess what? /ges wɒt/
I want to go. /aɪ wɒnt tə
  gəʊ/
Let's go together. /lets gəʊ
  təˈgeðər/
Of course /əv kɔːs/
What about you? /wɒt
  əˈbaʊt juː/

Unit 4

Family

aunt (n) /ɑːnt/
brother (n) /ˈbrʌðər/
children (n) /ˈtʃɪldrən/
cousin (n) /ˈkʌzən/
dad (n) /dæd/
daughter (n) /ˈdɔːtər/
grandfather (n)
  /ˈgrænd,fɑːðər/
grandmother (n)
  /ˈgrænd,mʌðər/
grandparent (n)
  /ˈgrænd,peərənt/
mum (n) /mʌm/
parent (n) /ˈpeərənt/
sister (n) /ˈsɪstər/
son (n) /sʌn/
uncle (n) /ˈʌŋkl/
wife (n) /waɪf/

Verbs

to be called /tə biː kɔːld/
finish /ˈfɪnɪʃ/
get /get/
give /gɪv/
go for a walk /gəʊ fərə
  wɔːk/
go shopping /gəʊ ˈʃɒpɪŋ/
have /hæv/
have a fight /hæv ə faɪt/
learn /lɜːn/
listen /ˈlɪsən/
live /lɪv/
look after /lʊk ˈɑːftər/
same /seɪm/
sell /sel/
speak /spiːk/
stop /stɒp/

study /ˈstʌdi/
watch /wɒtʃ/
write /raɪt/

Nouns

bank /bæŋk/
bicycle /ˈbaɪsɪkl/
cartoon /kɑːˈtuːn/
colour TV /ˈkʌlər ,tiːˈviː/
dishwasher /ˈdɪʃ,wɒʃər/
drink /drɪŋk/
garden /ˈgɑːdən/
hobby /ˈhɒbi/
hospital /ˈhɒspɪtəl/
house /haʊs/
job /dʒɒb/
letter /ˈletər/
magic /ˈmædʒɪk/
newspaper /ˈnjuːs,peɪpər/
north /nɔːθ/
nurse /nɜːs/
road /rəʊd/
shop /ʃɒp/
south /saʊθ/
sweet /swiːt/
teenager /ˈtiːn,eɪdʒər/
town /taʊn/
washing machine /ˈwɒʃɪŋ
  məˈʃiːn/
weekend /,wiːkˈend/
wizard /ˈwɪzəd/
work /wɜːk/
writer /ˈraɪtər/

Adjectives

dead /ded/
famous /ˈfeɪməs/
happy /ˈhæpi/
part time /paːt taɪm/
typical /ˈtɪpɪkəl/
unhappy /ʌnˈhæpi/

Prepositions

near /nɪər/

Unit 5

Places in towns

bookshop (n) /ˈbʊkʃɒp/
café (n) /ˈkæfeɪ/
chemist (n) /ˈkemɪst/
city centre (n) /ˈsɪti ˈsentər/
high street (n) /haɪ striːt/
library (n) /ˈlaɪbrəri/
newsagent (n)
  /ˈnjuːz,eɪdʒənt/
park (n) /pɑːk/
post office (n) /pəʊst ˈɒfɪs/
railway station (n) /ˈreɪlweɪ

ˈsteɪʃən/
street market (n) /striːt
  ˈmɑːkɪt/
supermarket (n)
  /ˈsuːpə,mɑːkɪt/
university (n)
  /,juːnɪˈvɜːsəti/

Verbs

ask /ɑːsk/
buy /baɪ/
catch /kætʃ/
change /tʃeɪndʒ/
do /duː/
excuse (me) /ɪkˈskjuːz/
happen /ˈhæpən/
look at /lʊk æt/
pay /peɪ/
send /send/
sit /sɪt/
start /stɑːt/
take /teɪk/
try /traɪ/
turn /tɜːn/
visit /ˈvɪzɪt/
wait /weɪt/

Nouns

air /eər/
biology /baɪˈɒlədʒi/
building /ˈbɪldɪŋ/
clothes /kləʊðz/
collection /kəˈlekʃən/
dinosaur /ˈdaɪnəsɔːr/
directions /dɪˈrekʃənz/
flight /flaɪt/
food /fuːd/
history /ˈhɪstəri/
hour /aʊər/
idea /aɪˈdɪə/
leader /ˈliːdər/
magazine /,mægəˈziːn/
milk /mɪlk/
minute /ˈmɪnɪt/
money /ˈmʌni/
opinion /əˈpɪnjən/
parcel /ˈpɑːsəl/
river boat /ˈrɪvər bəʊt/
shampoo /ʃæmˈpuː/
shoe /ʃuː/
sight /saɪt/
stamp /stæmp/
tour /tʊər/
tourist /ˈtʊərɪst/
travel card /ˈtrævəl kɑːd/
trip /trɪp/
underground line/train
  /ˈʌndəgraʊnd laɪn
  treɪn/
world /wɜːld/

Adjectives

beautiful /ˈbjuːtɪfəl/
different /ˈdɪfərənt/
fashionable /ˈfæʃənəbl/
natural /ˈnætʃərəl/
stupid /ˈstjuːpɪd/
young /jʌŋ/

Prepositions

around /əˈraʊnd/
behind /bɪˈhaɪnd/
between /bɪˈtwiːn/
down /daʊn/
in front of /ɪn frʌnt ɒv/
into /ˈɪntuː/
next to /nekst tuː/
opposite /ˈɒpəzɪt/

Everyday English

Are you sure? /ɑːr juː ʃɔːr/
I have no idea. /aɪ hæv nəʊ
  aɪˈdɪə/
Wait a minute. /weɪt ə
  ˈmɪnɪt/
You're welcome. /jɔːr
  ˈwelkəm/

Unit 6

Colours

beige (adj) /beɪʒ/
black (adj) /blæk/
blue (adj) /bluː/
brown (adj) /braʊn/
green (adj) /griːn/
grey (adj) /greɪ/
orange (adj) /ˈɒrɪndʒ/
pink (adj) /pɪŋk/
purple (adj) /ˈpɜːpl/
red (adj) /red/
white (adj) /waɪt/
yellow (adj) /ˈjeləʊ/

Parts of the body

arm (n) /ɑːm/
ear (n) /ɪər/
eye (n) /aɪ/
face (n) /feɪs/
finger (n) /ˈfɪŋgər/
foot (n) /fʊt/
hand (n) /hænd/
hair (n) /heər/
leg (n) /leg/
mouth (n) /maʊθ/
nose (n) /nəʊz/
thumb (n) /θʌm/

Pets

budgie (n) /'bʌdʒi/
collar (n) /'kɒlər/
guinea-pig (n) /'gɪni pɪg/
hamster (n) /'hæmpstər/
lead (n) /liːd/
lizard (n) /'lɪzəd/
owner (n) /'əʊnər/
rabbit (n) /'ræbɪt/
snake (n) /sneɪk/
spider (n) /'spaɪdər/

Verbs

break /breɪk/
destroy /dɪ'strɔɪ/
drive /draɪv/
have got /hæv gɒt/
repeat /rɪ'piːt/
spend /spend/
use /juːz/
wear /weər/

Nouns

age /eɪdʒ/
banana /bə'nɑːnə/
bed /bed/
chimpanzee /,tʃɪmpæn'ziː/
Christmas /'krɪsməs/
DNA /,diːen'eɪ/
DVD player /,diːviː'diː 'pleɪər/
electrical equipment /ɪ'lektrɪkəl ɪ'kwɪpmənt/
first name /'fɜːst neɪm/
forest /'fɒrɪst/
glasses /'glɑːsɪz/
hairstyle /'heəstaɪl/
home /həʊm/
membership form /'membəʃɪp fɔːm/
practice /'præktɪs/
smile /smaɪl/
stereo /'steriəʊ/
surname /'sɜːneɪm/
verb /vɜːb/
video store /'vɪdiəʊ stɔːr/

Adjectives

blonde /blɒnd/
curly /'kɜːli/
dark /dɑːk/
exotic /ɪg'zɒtɪk/
fair /feər/
good-looking /,gʊd'lʊkɪŋ/
intelligent /ɪn'telɪdʒənt/
little /'lɪtl/
long /lɒŋ/
luxury /'lʌkʃəri/
medium-length /'miːdiəm leŋkθ/
nice /naɪs/

practical /'præktɪkəl/
short /ʃɔːt/
similar /'sɪmɪlər/
straight /streɪt/
wavy /'weɪvi/
wrong /rɒŋ/

Question words

Why /waɪ/

Unit 7

Food

apple (n) /'æpl/
beef (n) /biːf/
bread (n) /bred/
burger (n) /'bɜːgər/
carrot (n) /'kærət/
cheese (n) /tʃiːz/
chicken (n) /'tʃɪkɪn/
chips (n) /tʃɪps/
dessert (n) /dɪ'zɜːt/
egg (n) /eg/
fruit (n) /fruːt/
grape (n) /greɪp/
honey (n) /'hʌni/
ice cream (n) /,aɪs'kriːm/
lamb (n) /læm/
lasagne (n) /lə'zænjə/
lettuce (n) /'letɪs/
mayonnaise (n) /,meɪə'neɪz/
meat (n) /miːt/
mousse (n) /muːs/
mushroom (n) /'mʌʃrʊm/
mustard (n) /'mʌstəd/
onion (n) /'ʌnjən/
orange (n) /'ɒrɪndʒ/
pâté (n) /'pæ'teɪ/
pie (n) /paɪ/
potato (n) /pə'teɪtəʊ/
rice (n) /raɪs/
roast lamb (n) /rəʊst læm/
salad (n) /'sæləd/
salt (n) /sɔːlt/
soup (n) /suːp/
steak (n) /steɪk/
strawberry (n) /'strɔːbəri/
sugar (n) /'ʃʊgər/
toast (n) /təʊst/
tomato (n) /tə'mɑːtəʊ/
vegetable (n) /'vedʒtəbl/
vinegar (n) /'vɪnɪgər/

Drink

cola (n) /'kəʊlə/
juice (n) /dʒuːs/
lemonade (n) /,lemə'neɪd/
tea (n) /tiː/
water (n) /'wɔːtər/

In a restaurant

fast food place (n) /fɑːst fuːd pleɪs/
lunchtime (n, adj) /'lʌntʃtaɪm/
main course (n) /meɪn kɔːs/
meal (n) /miːl/
menu (n) /'menjuː/
starter (n) /'stɑːtər/
waiter (n) /'weɪtər/

Verbs

arrive /ə'raɪv/
eat /iːt/
hate /heɪt/
order /'ɔːdər/
stay /steɪ/
tell /tel/

Nouns

alligator /'ælɪgeɪtər/
bus /bʌs/
day /deɪ/
exercise /'eksəsaɪz/
grasshopper /'grɑːs,hɒpər/
grocery /'grəʊsəri/
kangaroo /,kæŋgə'ruː/
kilo /'kiːləʊ/
month /mʌnθ/
rattlesnake /'rætlsneɪk/
selection /sɪ'lekʃən/
snail /sneɪl/

Adjectives

delicious /dɪ'lɪʃəs/
disgusting /dɪs'gʌstɪŋ/
fresh /freʃ/
hungry /'hʌngri/
lovely /'lʌvli/
ready /'redi/
special /'speʃəl/
strange /streɪndʒ/
true /truː/

Everyday English

Do you think so? /də jə θɪŋk səʊ/
I'm really hungry. /aɪm 'rɪəli 'hʌngri/
Really? /'rɪəli/
What's wrong? /wɒts rɒŋ/

Unit 8

Adverbs of frequency

always /'ɔːlweɪz/
every day/week/month/year /'evri deɪ wiːk mʌnθ jɪər/

hardly ever /'hɑːdli 'evər/
never /'nevər/
often /'ɒfən/
once a day/week/month/year /wʌns ə deɪ wiːk mʌnθ jɪər/
sometimes /'sʌmtaɪmz/
twice a day/week/month/year /twaɪs ə deɪ wiːk mʌnθ jɪər/
usually /'juːʒəli/

TV programmes

cartoon (n) /kɑː'tuːn/
chat show (n) /tʃæt ʃəʊ/
comedy programme (n) /'kɒmədi 'prəʊgræm/
documentary (n) /,dɒkjə'mentəri/
game show (n) /geɪm ʃəʊ/
school programme (n) /skuːl 'prəʊgræm/
soap opera /'səʊp,ɒpərə/
sports programme (n) /spɔːts 'prəʊgræm/
the news (n) /ðə njuːz/

Days of the week

Monday /'mʌndeɪ/
Tuesday /'tjuːzdeɪ/
Wednesday /'wenzdeɪ/
Thursday /'θɜːzdeɪ/
Friday /'fraɪdeɪ/
Saturday /'sætədeɪ/
Sunday /'sʌndeɪ/

Verbs

check /tʃek/
dance /dɑːns/
get up /get 'ʌp/
go swimming /gəʊ 'swɪmɪŋ/
sing /sɪŋ/
talk /tɔːk/

Nouns

breakfast /'brekfəst/
comedy /'kɒmədi/
dinner /'dɪnər/
electricity /,elɪk'trɪsəti/
email /'iːmeɪl/
evening /'iːvənɪŋ/
farm /fɑːm/
fish /fɪʃ/
interview /'ɪntəvjuː/
kilometre /kɪ'lɒmɪtər/
lesson /'lesən/
lunch /lʌntʃ/
radio /'reɪdiəʊ/

Adjectives

funny /ˈfʌni/
simple /ˈsɪmpl/
traditional /trəˈdɪʃəŋəl/

Unit 9

Adjectives to describe feelings

angry /ˈæŋgri/
bored /bɔːd/
confused /kənˈfjuːzd/
excited /ɪkˈsaɪtɪd/
sad /sæd/
scared /skeəd/
worried /ˈwʌrid/

Verbs

call /kɔːl/
close /kləʊz/
contact /ˈkɒntækt/
cry /kraɪ/
feel /fiːl/
forget /fəˈget/
go away /gəʊ əˈweɪ/
hang on (a minute) /hæŋ ɒn/
hear /hɪər/
join /dʒɔɪn/
laugh /lɑːf/
leave /liːv/
mail /meɪl/
miss /mɪs/
need /niːd/
park /pɑːk/
shout /ʃaʊt/
sleep /sliːp/
sound /saʊnd/
walk /wɔːk/

Nouns

boyfriend /ˈbɔɪfrend/
door /dɔːr/
grass /grɑːs/
girlfriend /ˈgɜːlfrend/
heart /hɑːt/
holiday /ˈhɒlədeɪ/
match /mætʃ/
mom /mɒm/
night /naɪt/
noise /nɔɪz/
team /tiːm/
test /test/

Adjectives

alone /əˈləʊn/
fancy /ˈfænsi/
final /ˈfaɪnəl/
fine /faɪn/

fun /fʌn/
late /leɪt/

Everyday English

I miss (San Francisco). /aɪ mɪs/
She's fine. /ʃiːz faɪn/
What's the matter? /wɒts ðə ˈmætər/

Unit 10

Sports

American football (n) /əˈmerɪkən ˈfʊtbɔːl/
basketball (n) /ˈbɑːskɪtbɔːl/
cricket (n) /ˈkrɪkɪt/
cycling (n) /ˈsaɪklɪŋ/
gymnastics (n) /dʒɪmˈnæstɪks/
hockey (n) /ˈhɒki/
netball (n) /ˈnetbɔːl/
riding (n) /ˈraɪdɪŋ/
rollerblading (n) /ˈrəʊləˌbleɪdɪŋ/
rugby (n) /ˈrʌgbi/
running (n) /ˈrʌnɪŋ/
soccer (n) /ˈsɒkər/
swimming (n) /ˈswɪmɪŋ/
triathlon (n) /traɪˈæθlɒn/

Verbs

count /kaʊnt/
cycle /ˈsaɪkl/
draw /drɔː/
find out /faɪnd aʊt/
hop /hɒp/
juggle /ˈdʒʌgl/
lie /laɪ/
pull /pʊl/
push /pʊʃ/
run /rʌn/
seem /siːm/
ski /skiː/
snowboard /ˈsnəʊbɔːd/
support /səˈpɔːt/
swim /swɪm/
take part /teɪk ˈpɑːt/
win /wɪn/

Nouns

bike /baɪk/
boat /bəʊt/
camel /ˈkæməl/
cerebral palsy /ˈserəbrəl ˈpɔːlzi/

Europe /ˈjʊərəp/
fact /fækt/
front /frʌnt/
guitar /gɪˈtɑːr/
member /ˈmembər/
oxygen /ˈɒksɪdʒən/
PE (physical education) /ˌpiːˈiː/
piano /pɪˈænəʊ/
race /reɪs/
sea /siː/
seat /siːt/
second /ˈsekənd/
sports hall /spɔːts hɔːl/
student /ˈstjuːdənt/
survey /ˈsɜːveɪ/
teenager /ˈtiːnˌeɪdʒər/
violin /ˌvaɪəˈlɪn/
wheelchair /ˈwiːltʃeər/
winter /ˈwɪntər/
worm /wɜːm/

Adjectives

cold /kəʊld/
free /friː/
local /ˈləʊkəl/
wet /wet/

Adverbs

quite /kwaɪt/
(very) well /wel/

Prepositions

against /əˈgenst/
outside /ˌaʊtˈsaɪd/
under /ˈʌndər/

Unit 11

House and furniture

armchair (n) /ˈɑːmtʃeər/
bathroom (n) /ˈbɑːθrʊm/
bedroom (n) /ˈbedrʊm/
cooker (n) /ˈkʊkər/
dining room (n) /ˈdaɪnɪŋ ruːm/
fridge (n) /frɪdʒ/
hall (n) /hɔːl/
kitchen (n) /ˈkɪtʃɪn/
living room (n) /ˈlɪvɪŋ ruːm/
roof (n) /ruːf/
shower (n) /ˈʃaʊər/
sofa (n) /ˈsəʊfə/

swimming pool (n) /ˈswɪmɪŋ puːl/
table (n) /ˈteɪbl/
toilet (n) /ˈtɔɪlət/

Weather

cloudy /ˈklaʊdi/
raining /ˈreɪnɪŋ/
sunny /ˈsʌni/
warm /wɔːm/

Verbs

babysit /ˈbeɪbɪsɪt/
clean /kliːn/
come /kʌm/
have a good/great time /hæv ə gʊd greɪt taɪm/
hope /həʊp/
make /meɪk/
rain /reɪn/
take a picture /teɪk ə ˈpɪktʃər/

Nouns

ball /bɔːl/
bath /bɑːθ/
beach /biːtʃ/
flat /flæt/
Maths /mæθs/
milkshake /mɪlk ʃeɪk/
party /ˈpɑːti/
sun /sʌn/
teeth (plural of tooth) /tiːθ/
weather /ˈweðər/

Everyday English

Come round to my place. /kʌm raʊnd tə maɪ pleɪs/
I'm on my way. /aɪm ɒn maɪ weɪ/
Nothing much. /ˈnʌθɪŋ mʌtʃ/
See you (soon). /siː juː/
What are you up to? /wɒt ɑːr juː ʌp tuː/